INVADENOLA.COM | 1

Y0-DFI-062

INTRO

featuring famous Blaxploitation actor Fred Williamson; you will learn the Muslim roots of an Urban Outfitters trend; and experience one writer's near breakup with New Orleans.

I know that sounds ridiculous, but it's true. One day after watching an episode of "The Hills," I decided MTV had failed us, and vowed to prove that millennials have the power to change the world in a positive way.

Since December 2009, InvadeNOLA has delivered a weekly digital magazine that serves as the voice of New Orleans: authentic, multicultural, and irreverent. But now we're finally going analog with our first printed book. I wanted to do something a little more tangible. Something you could wrap your fingers around.

While the internet displays your words to the masses, there is something magical about printed words on paper. In this book, you will read one writer's search for a *Playgirl* magazine

It's our personal testament of sex, music, and culture from the perspective of some pretty awesome millennials. But the real magic is that we did it ourselves for ourselves, funded by people who genuinely believe in the power of independent media.

So thanks to you for purchasing. Thanks to these wonderful writers. And thanks to everyone who had the audacity to believe in a ridiculous 25-year-old who has big dreams.

love.justin

Using Kickstarter.com, we raised $3,500 from 105 people in 35 days. Without these guys, this book wouldn't be possible. Thank you.

Kat Haro	Sloane Berrent	Peter Bodenheimer
Chris Schultz	Kezia Kamenetz	David Stuckey
Angela	Vignette Ching	Brittany
Victoria Adams	Pho Hoa Restaurant	Laura
Ashley	Patricia Quinn	Nathan Martin
Lauren Domino	Constance Young	Mike Baldwin
Jeff Schwartz	Jessica Rohloff	Catherine
Courtney Sutherby	Rebecca Hb.	Ray Nichols
Avram	Michael Goldman	Barrett Macgowan
Britt	Maureen Bongiovanni	Erick Greene
Nevl	Stephanie Moody	Val McKay
Karen Buck	CEDRIC HARRIS	Elizabeth McCarthy
Moni	Sara Silvestri	Earl Scioneaux
Rachel Puckett	Aneka	Ann Bernard
Addie King	Brandon Sutton	Matthew Rosenthal
Tara	Tatanisha Harris	Lindsay Glatz
Emma	Kerry	M Trevor Acy
David Robinson-Morris	Joy Guerin	C. Gammill
John Pucci	Jeremy Braud	Ahmane' Glover
Meg Brogan	Alisha	Alexandra Grant
Christopher Payne	Megan Anne	Michelle Currica
Jewel Constance	Casey Moore	Mark
Serina Phoenix	Andrew Larimer	Connie S.
Marie Bourgeois	Bryce	
James C.	Jason Otis	
Erin Burns	Bill Kappel	
Candace W.	Lori Archer	
Marc LaPorte	Amy Jett	
Bridge for Emerging Contemporary Art	Jaira	
	LeeAnn	
Champ Superstar	Clare	
sergio padilla	Dorothy Ball	
What's my mutha f****** name, Behar!	Braden Piper	
	Tung Bach Ly	
Hope King	Tom Futrell	
Alaina Buzas	Ashley Thomas	
Jamie Donnelly	Dee Brown	
James Martin	Melissa A. Weber	
Thuy Le	Good Rockin RJ	
Zach	Carrie Harris	
Tim Soslow	Charles Lumar	

CONTENTS

006 Contributors

009 In the Next Decade I Predict

020 Why New Orleans
    Rosalie Cohn

023 Please Trust Your Server
    Hank Sweeny

026 My Secret Boyfriend
    PJ Doser

030 Oh, Mr. Williamson
    Jewel Bush

034 Ugly Jaira
    Jaira Harrington

040 My Secret Neighborhood
    Cate Root

044 To Keep or not to Keep
    Braden Piper

046 Last Night the DJ Saved my Life
    Lizzie Ford-Madrid

050 Redefining Secrets
    Jené Liggins

052 Cubicle
    Kat Haro

054 She. It. Us. Them.
    Ashley Chapman

060 Its the End of the World
    PJ Doser

063 Album Review
    Alex Palumbo Green

066 Interview: Blair McClain Johnson

070 Accessorizing Politically
    Taslim Van Hattum

076 Grownups Don't Let Grownups Pass on STDs
    Karen Alise

079 Pee After Sex
    Karen Alise

084 Broke Ass Homeowner: Decor on a Budget
    Sarah Andert

088 Interview: Bionica
    Laura Klein

092 Dear Hipster Male
    Justin Shiels

094 Fat in Thin Times
    Karen Alise

098 Blogging is Dead
    Justin Shiels

100 Last Call
    Ashley Chapman

102 Dometic
    Anna Farinas

104 Looking for Love in all the Wrong Places
    Cate Root

CONTRIBUTORS

KAREN ALISE is a young writer born in Boston, now writing from Atlanta. You can follow her at www.lovealise.com or @xlovealise on Twitter.

SARAH ANDERT grew up in Minnesota, from whence she departed a decade ago to complete her BA and MA in English at Tulane. She's currently employed at the Center for Public Service as an internship coordinator and is now working on an Environmental Studies degree. She loves to play dress up and lives for New Orleans's countless opportunities to costume, parade, and party.

JEWEL BUSH is journalist/writer who has received numerous accolades for her work, including distinctions from The New York Times Regional Media Group, Louisiana Press Association, and American Association of Sunday and Feature Editors. The New Orleans native has freelanced for the *Washington Post* and the *Times-Picayune;* and is an alumna of the Callaloo Creative Writing Workshop and Voices of Our Nation Foundation Writers of Color Workshop.

ASHLEY CHAPMAN is a beautifully human Georgia native who has called New Orleans home for the past five years. She enjoys reading, partying, and big windows.

ROSALIE COHN is a lover of music, adventures, yoga and strange people. A Michigan native, she now calls New Orleans home.

PJ DOSER, raised in the wilds of Montana by Milo and Otis, was a feral child until the age of the three. Two years of rehabilitation later and a brief appearance on "Oprah," she set out to find the world's best foster parents. This experience was documented in the major motion picture "North" starring Elijah Wood. All that and more have made PJ into the hermit she is today. She is pleased as punch to write for InvadeNOLA and have contact with the outside world that is not therapist appointed.

ANNA FARINAS is a high school English teacher in Dallas. She loves the smell of freshly sharpened pencils, naps, and duck sauce.

KAT HARO is a public relations gal turned jack-of-all-communications-based-trades. Her life in cubicles recently ended when she was given an office with a real door. It may be enclosed, but these walls are still thin. Folks, beware.

JAIRA J. HARRINGTON is a PhD student in the Department of Political Science at the University of Chicago. Her major subfield is Comparative Politics with a regional focus on Brazil. Her current interests include Red Vines licorice, Portuguese, political blogs, works by Richard Wright, and putting the "bad" in Badminton.

MCCLAIN JOHNSON is a freelance writer and interviewer originally from Kansas City, Missouri. His work can be viewed on his website mcclainjohnson.com.

LAUREN KLEIN is originally from Chicago and has lived in New Orleans for the last three years and counting. She is an English major at the University of New Orleans and a jazz fanatic.

JENE' LIGGINS is a native of Baton Rouge and has lived in New Orleans since 2001. She likes traveling, being a tourist in her own city, and good music, especially Earth, Wind and Fire and Erykah Badu.

ALEX PALUMBO-GREEN is a New Orleanian and part time contributing writer to InvadeNola. He hopes that one day he will be able to utter the phrase "I tickled Dr. Dre and lived to tell the tale."

BRADEN PIPER is a creative professional. If you'd like to learn more, visit his website at www.bgpiper.com.

JUSTIN SHIELS is a writer, designer, and thinker who's attempting to become more human every day.

TASLIM VAN HATTUM, originally from Dar al Islam, a self-sufficient Muslim community in the mountains of Northern New Mexico and currently a resident of New Orleans, is a social worker and public health professional specializing in Maternal and Child Health and Geriatrics.

IN THE NEXT DECADE I PREDICT...

With the dawning of a new decade, the staff of InvadeNOLA took some time out to poll the populace on their predictions for the next ten years. Below you will find an interesting look into the mind of the millennial. From health to fashion, we expect some major changes, challenges, and opportunities to arise. **Baby boomers, you have been warned.**

Data-driven marketing will prevail. The web will become even more social. And everything online will be customizable.

Addie

Great heights in the apex of excitement and lowest of the lows in the disasters yet to come.

Erik

Music genres will be thing of the past. Rock will be the new pop.

Charles

We'll definitely get a female president. California is due for a big earthquake (that's morbid though).

Clark

Gay marriage will be legalized… as will marijuana. At least in some states.

Cat

The U.S. is gonna face some real hardships that will humble our country and get the rest of the world to like us more because of our new attitude.

Michael

All things corporate will die...

Mahoganygirl

I predict fashion will repeat the '30s, unemployment will go to 11 percent, and we still won't have hovercrafts.

will

I'd say that you are going to start seeing our generation focusing on building companies around real products instead of just services or social networking. It's going to be less lucrative to ship things, so more and more goods are going to be made in the States. There will be major manufacturing like infrastructure and green energy.

Austin

Health studies will show all the steroids they put in meat are making us sick.

Lauren

WHY NEW ORLEANS?

ROSALIE COHN

I spent my first Christmas Eve in New Orleans sitting, merrily enough, alone at a bar in the Irish Channel. By the time I'd ordered my second vodka soda, I'd become immersed in conversation with the two local women sitting next to me. As it turned out, they had a lot to say.

New Orleans, they told me, would either shower you with love and luck or chew you up and spit you out, broken and hurting. Treat the city well, they said, and she will do the same for you.

My time in New Orleans has taught me that these women were right. A place of self-discovery and strange opportunities, New Orleans is what you make of it. As you get to know New Orleans and find your place here, here are a few suggestions:

START SMALL.
New Orleans is a city of neighborhoods. Get to know yours. Each neighborhood in the city has its own personality, its own idiosyncrasies and hidden gems. Make it a habit to sit on your porch

and enjoy a good book, creating the opportunity to talk with those that live nearest you. Frequent your neighborhood coffee shop, become a regular at your neighborhood bar, and take your dog to your neighborhood park. Begin by carving out a niche in the space closest to your home, and then hop on a bicycle and get to know every other neighborhood in New Orleans.

GO OUTSIDE.

New Orleans is very car-friendly, but the best way to get to know the city is on a bike. Bike everywhere, and explore Lakeshore Drive and the 22-mile trail atop the Mississippi River levee. Both City Park and Audubon Park are great spots not only to bike, but to run, picnic and dream. Canoe or kayak along Bayou St. John. On a hazy spring or fall afternoon, there is nothing better than a barbeque at the Fly (named after a nearly forgotten butterfly-shaped shelter that was constructed in the 1960s) with friends. Take the free ferry across the Mississippi to Algiers Point, and enjoy a dreamlike view of the Crescent City. The romantic aesthetics of our home – the murky Mississippi, Crayola-colored houses, massive oaks embraced by Spanish moss – are longstanding

muses to famed playwrights, authors and musicians. Let New Orleans become your muse as well.

SOAK UP THE MUSIC.

In New Orleans, you can enjoy sublimely talented musicians in intimate settings every day, oftentimes for free. The birthplace of jazz, New Orleans also boasts a thriving hip-hop community, an undercover indie scene, and some of the weirdest musicians you will ever encounter. Program WWOZ 90.7 FM on your radio, and listen online at www.wwoz.org. Dig through crates at Domino Sound, Jim Russell Records, the Louisiana Music Factory and Euclid Records. For the best live music, head to Tipitina's, House of Blues, One Eyed Jacks, Circle Bar, AllWays Lounge, Maple Leaf, Saturn Bar, The Saint, Hi-Ho Lounge, Mimi's in the Marigny, The Howlin' Wolf, Republic, and anywhere on Frenchmen Street. If you dig it, get into it and support it.

BASK IN ART AND CULTURE.

The blossoming art scene in New Orleans is centered in the CBD, but also has hubs in the Bywater, French Quarter and Uptown. White Linen Night, Dirty Linen Night, Art for Art's Sake and Jammin' on Julia are among the biggest annual art events, and monthly gallery openings and art walks happen on the first Saturday of the month on Julia Street and the second Saturday of the month on St. Claude Avenue. The New Orleans Museum of Art is free to all on Wednesdays, and The Ogden Museum of Southern Art is free to Louisiana residents on Thursdays (also check out Ogden's After Hours concert series.) The Ashé Cultural Arts Center, Prytania Theatre and the Zeitgeist Multi-Disciplinary Arts Center host film screenings and cultural events covering the wackiest of topics. Keep your eyes and ears open, and you will discover art in every inch of the city.

PARTICIPATE.
Dance at live shows. Join in second lines. Don wigs, glitter, and the wildest getup possible during Mardi Gras. New Orleans is a participatory place, and everything is more fun when you're a part of it. There is always a reason to celebrate here, and you will quickly learn that there is a festival for everything. While Jazz Fest, French Quarter Fest, Po-Boy Fest, Satchmo SummerFest, Bayou Boogaloo and Mirliton Fest are among the cream of the crop, it is in your best interest to attend as many festivals as possible. As you immerse yourself in the decadence of our city, you will commonly find yourself at a parade, second line, or festival thinking, "everywhere else it's Sunday," and remember with a vengeance why you chose to call New Orleans home.

It's been nearly two years since my vodka-soaked Christmas Eve, and my mind still ponders the wisdom and superstition of my barstool friends. As I think back to our conversation, I realize that it is not only my relationship with New Orleans, but also my relationships with the New Orleanians I've met, and the New Orleanian I've become, that have defined my experience here.

Bob Dylan once wrote, "New Orleans, unlike a lot of those places you go back to and that don't have the magic anymore, still has got it. Night can swallow you up, yet none of it touches you. Around any corner, there's a promise of something daring and ideal and things are just getting going." Dylan was right. For newcomers to the Crescent City, an exciting adventure lies ahead. For as you begin to discover New Orleans, you will, in turn, discover magic, and discover yourself. 💣

PLEASE TRUST YOUR SERVER

HANK SWEENEY

Please, please, please. When you are there in the fancy chain restaurant, sitting in your booth—of course you had to squish your family of seven into the round booth in the corner that is meant for five because, I mean, really, who sits in chairs anymore?—and you realize that something in the restaurant is not quite exactly how you remember it, whether it be the menu or the drink specials or the amount of light in the room, please trust your server when he says that you're wrong.

For four of the most miserable months of my entire life, I worked at Applebee's in Metairie. There are a multitude of reasons to explain my misery, but out of the respect I have for my former bosses and many of my former colleagues (by respect, I mean that I have removed you from my memory thanks to magnanimous servings of Jameson), I am going to let them off the hook for now and, for the time being, focus on the customer.

I mean the "guests."

No, wait, I mean "our friends and family."

Our friends and family, please, trust your server. We are not all incompetent. We may be drunk and more likely severely hung over thanks to the gloriously-across-the-street-from-Applebee's Bottom Line Bar & Grill ("Lemme get a tuna steak. Rare. Did I say rare? Make it raw. And five pints of Guinness. No, six! And four shots! And, oh, lemme get a martini too. And some chili fries. Aw, shit, I spent all of my tips for the night. Good thing I have work again at ten-thirty a.m. That's in two hours, you say?").

But we are not incompetent. When you demand that dessert should come with your 2 For $20 Meal, and I explain, politely I'm sure, that the 2 for $20 at Applebee's does not come with a dessert (that's Chili's!), please do not ask to see the manager.

(On second thought, I take this back because any time I've ever seen anyone complain about anything, the complainer has always received a free dessert).

We, servers, are not lying to you. We don't have time to make up crazy lies and screw you out of desserts. We don't even want to lie to you. We just want to move to the next table and make sure everyone's happy. Because if someone is not happy, we get in trouble. And if we get in trouble, we might get written up in the black book of death. No one wants to be written up in the black book. Trust us. Working at Applebee's is embarrassing enough. Getting fired from Applebee's is downright humiliating.

I know that you remember being here only a couple days ago and chowing down on delicious sweet potato fries, but I am telling you that you were not. I have been here almost every day for the past four months, and we have not had sweet potato fries any of these days.

"But you have cream of broccoli soup every Saturday night. I remember."
I am very sorry, but you are wrong. Maybe you have had cream of broccoli soup every Saturday night, but we do not. And we never have.

It's okay. Don't be too hard on yourself. There are a lot of restaurants around here, and for the most part, they are all the same. They all have burgers and some sort of slimy, grilled chicken dish and dry, chewy steaks and frozen seafood shipped from Taiwan and also some rendition of the ridiculous spinach-and-artichoke dip that you think is healthy because you see the words "spinach" and "artichoke," but you fail to realize that it is full of cheese and cheese and more cheese. So I am not surprised that you have confused our menu with someone else's, and I forgive you. But when you do get confused, please trust your server. We are not all incompetent.

When you don't trust your server, you may order something that you are not going to like. As servers, we have nothing better to do in our spare time than to read the menus of our wonderful place of employment. We know what's on the menu and just about everything that is in each dish. We also know which dishes are enjoyable and which are God-awful (ahem, the Riblets. By the way, these are not just a cheaper version of baby back ribs). This is what happens when you don't trust your server. I promise you, this really happened:

Guest/Friend/Family: Excuse me, sir. [He called me sir!] "This Sizzling Chicken with Spicy Queso Blanco dish with the flaming apple next to it. Is that really spicy?

Server: Yes. It is very spicy. Thus, the flaming red apple beside it.

Guest/Friend/Family: Hmm. I don't really like spicy food.

Server: Well, you definitely shouldn't get that then. It's really spicy.

Guest/Friend/Family: Hmm. I might like it though. I like chicken. And I like cheese.

Server: Sir, if you don't like spicy food, you will not like this dish. It is very spicy. How about the Fiesta Lime Chicken instead?

Guest/Friend/Family: I'm gonna try it.

Twenty minutes later, my guest/friend/family was yelling at me: "This is really spicy! You didn't tell me it was really spicy! I can't even eat this!"

If you would like a superior dining experience (go to Brennan's!), please, please, please trust your server.

But more importantly—and I don't think enough people understand this—don't piss us off. Remember, we handle your food. 💣

MY SECRET BOYFRIEND

BY: PJ DOSER

I've got a secret.

Mike, my boyfriend of the last six years, well... he's not real. I'm not a crazy person with delusions of grandeur; I don't think I'll marry Robert Pattinson someday; and I only see my therapist on every first Wednesday. In all actuality, I'm simply an asshole.

The lie—well, secret (you lie to strangers; you keep secrets from friends)—started a balmy fall night my freshman year. Instead of admitting to my friends that I was tired of grinding my ass against strangers with ashy hands at frat parties, I lied and said I had a date with my imaginary lover. Honesty is overrated when you love friendship bracelets and want a BFF army large enough to protect a small developing nation.

In my defense, I do know a Mike. I sat next to him in fourth-grade French. My date with Mike was to be a one-off occurrence, but instead I pulled it out whenever I wanted to skip out on mandatory group fun. My made-up date turned into a full-blown imaginary relationship. After six years of good times eating Chinese takeout, watching bad movies, and catching up with soaps, we broke up. He wanted to get married and I just didn't see a future.

My secret served me well for so long I've decided to pay it forward and help you all do the same.

Don't want to go to the Creed reunion concert? "Mike just called. He's having a shitty week at work and just wants to talk." Want to skip sushi and sob stories, or helping someone move? "I already made plans with Mike and we don't get to see each often." Sure it makes you a little bit of a bad friend, but it works. No harm, no foul, no feeling hurt. Your friends are happy, you're happy.

Follow the steps below and prepare yourself for a relationship only Stephenie Meyer could write and months of skipping out on shit you really don't want to do.

STEP ONE: BACK STORY

You'll be bombarded with questions about your new love, and you need answers to satiate the masses. "How did you meet and why don't we know about him?" The answer's simple if they're people you didn't grow up with: he's from your hometown. You went to middle school with him, and

MY SECRET SERVED ME WELL FOR SO LONG I'VE DECIDED TO PAY IT FORWARD AND HELP YOU ALL DO THE SAME.

you were waiting until it was serious before you wanted everyone all up in your business. If you did grow up around these people, Craigslist or any other online dating site is always the answer. It's embarrassing enough that you don't have to go into detail. No one wants to go talk about their desperation. Your friends will let it slide.

STEP TWO: BEYONCÉ
Ringtones are essential in the process, as the bulk of relationship will take place through phone dates. Have a special ringtone for your imaginary lover. Pick someone who calls frequently, and change the name in your phone. My mom was labeled "Mike" for a fair amount of time. Whenever "Dangerously In Love" would ring out, I knew to take the call outside and prepare to discuss the amount of fiber in my diet.

STEP THREE: EXPLANATIONS
As your relationship progresses, people will wonder why they never see the lion to your lamb. The answer is simple: the United States Armed Forces. It explains long stretches of time apart and extreme mood swings. The mood swings come in handy. Let's say you're invited to watch a health care debate; you have plans with Mike. If this invitation suddenly shifts to watching a "Rock of Love" marathon and partaking in copious amounts of

recreational fun, "Mike totally just flipped on me, urgh why am I even with him? I just want to have fun and not think about him." Done and done. Always have explanations like this handy in case fun arises. You'll also have to explain why the bf isn't on Twitter, Facebook, and every other social networking site. He's an elitist and thinks these sites have only ruined human connection. Your friends will think he's a douche and talk about him behind your back. And that's better than to your face, it'll save you some precious excuses for a later date.

STEP FOUR: RUPAUL
"If you can't love yourself how the hell you gonna love anybody else." Prepare to spend lots of time by with the love of your life: yourself. I learned how to knit and also processed some deep emotional stuff. Not getting that Barbie Dream house with the elevator as a child took a hefty toll.

STEP FIVE: CONFESSIONS
All good things come to end, and eventually your big secret will too. You'll get sick of lying and end the fake relationship, or you'll get caught. In the midst of all the lies, it's time for truth. My personal truth is that my parents let me watch "Drop Dead Fred" too much as child and it completely changed the way I viewed relationships. We're all fucked up from childhood, and I just didn't know how to move on. I didn't have the pills Phoebe Cates had. At this point I cry a little, and pull out a bag of friendship bracelets. "Please still be my friend."

Image via flickr.com/photos/tinker-tailor

OH, MR. WILLIAMSON

BY: JEWEL BUSH

It started out as a Facebook rant about an eBay purchase gone awry. Then it turned into a public confession about an obsession that I had only recently revealed to those closest to me.

Ready?

I love Fred Williamson.

His name doesn't necessarily herald fanfare today, but the former pro footballer turned blaxploitation movie star was a sex symbol in the '70s. Well, he's still a sex symbol to me in the year 2009 (that's Fred Williamson circa 1973, NOT the Fred Williamson of 2009—I know, a bit confusing.

My second confession... I absolutely adore blaxploitation flicks. I seek out these movies. The more obscure the better. The more nudity, the better. The more drug use, the better. The more violence, the better. The dirtier the language, the better. The more terrible the acting, the better. To hell with political correctness when you can stick it to the man, run a scheme on a jive turkey, or seek revenge on a business associate who double-crossed you all while rocking over-the-top outfits, super-sized Afros and boogieing to the funkiest music of the time from the likes of Roy Ayers and Curtis Mayfield.

Segregation was over. Jim Crow flew the coop. Enter, blaxploitation. The storylines were dark and gritty and came at a time in American history when black folks were saying it loud: "I'm black and I'm proud!" and "I'm black and I'm poor" and "I'm black and I'm not going to take this anymore." The characters were badass

I DISCOVERED THAT HE POSED NUDE FOR PLAYGIRL IN 1973. I HAD TO HAVE THE ISSUE.

and oftentimes downtrodden but they reflected this bold, dynamic sentiment that was new to film. Moviegoers hadn't seen black people in roles of power and control before in cinema. Nor had they seen sensitive issues in the black community like crime, poverty, desperation, and the complexities of racism played out on the big screen.

Blaxploitation delivered. This cinematic period gave birth to classics like "Watermelon Man," "Space is the Place," "The Spook Who Sat By the Door," "Trick Baby" and my personal all-time favorites Pam Grier's "Coffy" and "Black Caesar," starring Fred Williamson. James Brown scored the entire soulful soundtrack for the 1973 movie. You know the music. It's been sampled by just about every rap artist from Ice-T to Das EFX to Trick Daddy. You definitely know the lyrics. They are some of the most quoted in hip hop: "Paid the cost to be the boss." This year, *Empire* magazine ranked "Black Caesar" as number 18 in its poll of the 20 Greatest Gangster Movies You've Probably Never Seen.

A few months ago, during one of my frequent Fred Williamson Google searches, I discovered that he posed nude for *Playgirl* in 1973. I had to have the issue. After a week of bidding on eBay—really, waiting for the auction to end —I took the prize uncontested. How could I be the only one checking for Fred Williamson? Nonetheless, I reveled in my good fortune, going home on my lunch break to check the mail.

I was ecstatic the day it came. I carefully flipped through the pages of the aged periodical waiting patiently for the glorious moment to see Fred Williamson nude in a magazine published before I was born. Yet there was no Fred Williamson centerfold. The pages were missing. I had been duped!

That's what I get for being a pervert, I thought.

I immediately fired off a nasty email to the seller while sharing my negative customer feedback with the eBay world and in a note on Facebook. My secret was out. I was in love with the Fred Williamson of 1973, and I bought a 36-year-old issue of *Playgirl* from eBay just to see him naked.

Luckily, the seller had more copies.

A week later, my second issue of the October 1973 issue of *Playgirl* arrived. The centerfold was intact this time, but I was still let-down. A shadowed side view of a derrière wasn't exactly

what I consider nudity. The styling for the shoot was all wrong too. Purple underwear, coral jogging pants—the pits! And whoever decided to pose Fred Williamson to pose with a white kitten should have been flogged.

Fred Williamson is still dreamy to me, though. The Fred Williamson of 1973, that is. We all need a vice. 💣

UGLY JAIRA

BY: JAIRA HARRINGTON

Author's note: This story was initially sent to some of my friends via email. I have yet to embrace blogging or Tweeting, and, at the hazard of losing a personal touch, I cling to emails and snail mail for dear life. JH

This year, I went to a Halloween party at a friend of a good friend's house. I've known this strapping young lad for years, and he knew some people who were throwing a shindig. They promised heavy quantities of Gucci Mane ("brrr!"). It sounded like fun.

A few hours before the event, I was at a store laboring over what I ought to wear as a costume. As I combed through the racks of typical 20-something female costumes — sexy cop, sexy firefighter, sexy zookeeper, sexy beluga whale complete with garter belt and handcuffs — I realized that none of these costumes quite captured my personality.

I thought I'd hit the jackpot when I stumbled upon a wig, fake braces, and red glasses — Ugly Betty (or in this case Ugly Jaira)!

I transformed instantly from being sensibly dressed and pretty normal to blue-brace-faced and four-eyed with clashing colors and patterns. I had unwittingly become the independent variable in my own social experiment: Given "Ugly Jaira" and either some or no prior knowledge of her background, connections to the party or social status, how would people choose to respond when given more information about the Jaira J. Harrington underneath the disguise?

tights and leopard-print ballet flats. If I didn't walk in tore up, I certainly felt shredded right then.

As I entered, most people were confused at why such a nerdy, awkwardly dressed girl would come to a house party with the young, professional and beautiful black elite.

Yet the hostesses were kind. They remarked on how thoughtful it was of

I THOUGHT I'D HIT THE JACKPOT WHEN I STUMBLED UPON A WIG, FAKE BRACES, AND RED GLASSES—UGLY BETTY (OR IN THIS CASE UGLY JAIRA)!

I didn't realize this until I got to the party, but I had dressed in a manner that was insufficiently extreme.

As I walked inside, I could feel eyes vertically burning through my red argyle sweater, yellow turtleneck, lime-green accessories, red plastic glasses, blue braces, and gray/black skirt, and horizontally ripping apart my textured

me to bring non-alcoholic beverages and table crackers to the house of someone that I didn't know personally. They were flattered. But even they were concerned about my attire. Early on, I found myself explaining to them that I was in costume as Ugly Betty. They seemed to be a bit relieved.

From that moment I realized that some people could have simply interpreted me as a poorly dressed, unfortunately uncoordinated young woman, which would have been fine. What unsettled me was the way in which some people treated me because of what I was wearing, and how their tune changed when they found out about who I really am.

Chicago is a little big city. Everybody knows everybody. So even though I didn't know the hostesses of the party, I knew some of people there from either the campus of the University of Chicago, Spelman-Morehouse, my high school, internship programs, or other Chicago-related connections. But still, the costume was just subtle enough that some people didn't get the joke. Others didn't watch "Ugly Betty."

I felt completely invisible. It was as if I were drop of geeky oil in a sea of social water—few people even wanted to interact with me. My good friend who invited me, however, was able to help me break the ice. I have never had this problem before!

He proudly began introducing me to people that I did not know, and shared my local, national, and international connections. Then, and only then, did strangers perk up. "Oh, you're from University of Chicago?" "Oh, a PhD student? Wow!" "Oh, Brazil! How exciting! I'm so jealous!" Ahem, status check on deck.

However, I felt more confident speaking to people because they displayed some interest. In a sense, I discussed my education much more than normal, because I felt like I had to compensate for my appearance. I caught myself doing it. From then on, I did the usual "Jaira." I just talked to whomever about whatever and enjoyed myself in the process.

I reconnected with folks who saw me speak on panels at school and participate in student activities. I reminded people about where we had met in the past at Spel-House or Kenwood Academy High School. But even after doing that, I found myself explaining away my costume. I had to justify my attendance and, to a certain extent, my existence.

My explanation settled the million dollar

question that no one dared to ask: "Why are you here?"

After a while, I was bold enough to inform a couple of the partygoers that they were a part of a social experiment and that they had wandered into my survey. Shock and embarrassment seeped onto their faces. They anxiously wondered if they had passed the test. Funny, because I felt as though I had failed as soon as I walked through the door. I quickly let them know I was kidding—sort of.

The male-female dynamic was interesting too. The party itself was male-dominated with few women (2—3:1). And, per usual, I started talking with some guys. No intentions, just chatting. And over time, I started getting the undivided attention of a few. A few unnamed (and otherwise unfamiliar) female sexy-(occupation here) attendees did not like the attention that Ugly Jaira was getting. So, how is it that some decided to distract the manfolk from the allure of the confident, goggle-eyed, brace-faced charmer? Go straight to the old default: show sum'n. Nothing to get that testosterone re-focused like an impromptu dance-off! Ok. That's my cue. Time to go. As I entered the elevator I wished some exiting partygoers a good time. I allowed the elevator doors to close and shrugged it off as research experience. From beginning to end, an interesting night.

Please don't get me wrong. It wasn't all bad. I had a crazy great time! I traded business cards, caught up with some of my good, good friends, and got my Gucci Mane fix—all in one night.

But I also learned so much about people that I had not anticipated. The part that I feared most about the Halloween party (other than the possible cross-contamination of sour cream dip and salsa, eww...) was that people might be more shallow than I had once thought. I didn't want to believe that it is true, but now I have some suggestive empirical evidence that this may be the case.

Sigh. 💣

IF YOU'RE NOT FAILING, YOU'RE NOT RISKING ENOUGH.

MORAL OF THE DAY

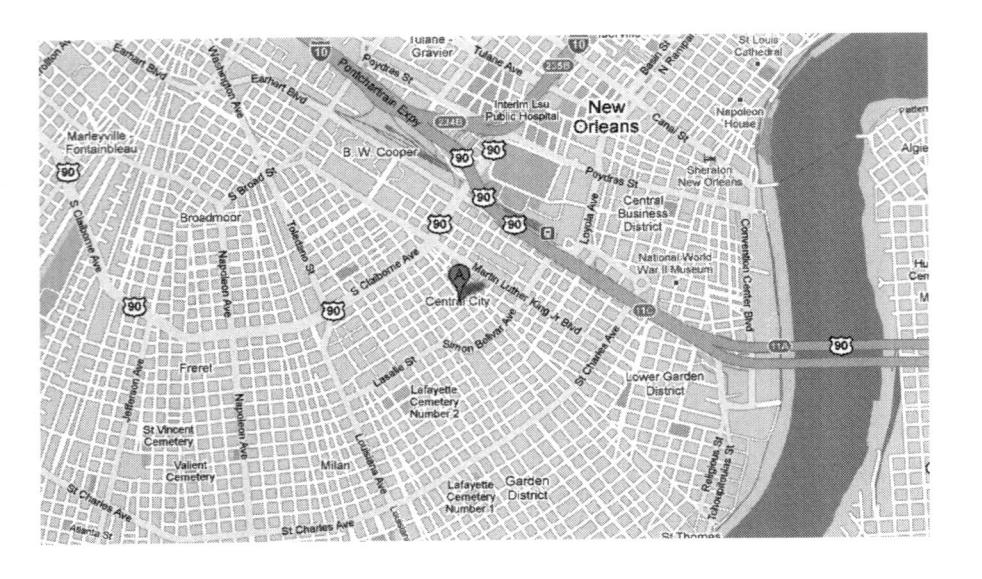

MY SECRET NEIGHBOR HOOD

CATE ROOT

Five teenagers were gunned down at the intersection of Josephine and Danneel streets in Central City, New Orleans, on June 17, 2006.

The incident triggered the deployment of National Guard troops to patrol the crime-ridden city. They stayed until February 2009. At the end of this year, I moved into an apartment two blocks from the site of the massacre.

THERE ARE PARADES AND MARDI GRAS INDIANS. THERE IS VIOLENCE AND DRUGS. BUT UNDER THE MUCK, THERE IS A COMMUNITY.

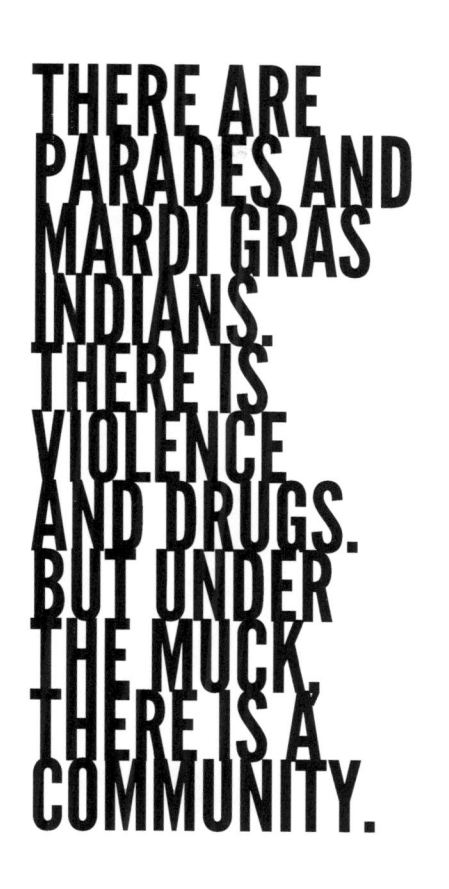

Central City is the part of town we like to gloss over. There are parades and Mardi Gras Indians. There is violence and drugs. But under the muck, there is a community. This historically black, working-class neighborhood gained prominence as a commercial district during the Jim Crow era, then declined over the past half century. Central City is an area that many New Orleanians try to avoid, ignore, or forget. As we continue avert our eyes, the artists' ensemble Mondo Bizarro has begun to tell us stories to remember this secret New Orleans.

Scattered around Central City are markers for the "I-Witness Central City" project. The Mondo Bizarro website shows a map of the twenty story locations and recommends a walking tour of story sites. In true New Orleans style, they're less sanitized than your traditional feel-good project. Saddi Khali talks about being chased by a six-foot-two cross-dressing prostitute, and Kirah Haubrich tells the story of how her neighbor intervened to stop a car theft—but ended up in handcuffs (he was apparently wearing a Hawaiian shirt and nothing else).

But most of the stories highlight the

strong sense of community that characterizes the neighborhood. Bernard Jones speaks about his ragtag childhood football team with their mismatched cleats, helmets, and jerseys. Above all, he stresses how important Central City is to him: "I still come back to my neighborhood no matter what I do in life."

It's not all bad, this Central City living. When people at work ask me where I live, I still sometimes itch for that euphemism, "Carondelet Corridor," but I stay true (mostly so they know they aren't paying me enough). People can say what they want about Central City. They can be afraid of it. They can make callous jokes about drive-by shootings and the drug trade. They can try to convince themselves that their own neighborhood is safer than mine. But the secret of this neighborhood is in its heartbeat, still pumping after all these years. The community persists, one person and one home at a time. Hopefully, someday I can add a good story to the "I-Witness Central City" project. Even if Central City is a "secret" part of New Orleans, at least it won't be forgotten. 💣

IS THIS WORTH SPENDING YOUR LIFE ON?

CAUSE IF ITS NOT, MAYBE ITS TIME TO MOVE ON.

MORAL OF THE DAY

Image via: http://www.flickr.com/photos/khywashere/

TO KEEP OR NOT TO KEEP

BRADEN PIPER

In this age of social networking—I'm increasingly fearing an internet brain implant that more efficiently updates my Twitter feed and Facebook status—I cant quite decide if I should tweet out the location of Singleton's po-boy shop or not. I feel like this is the same dilemma I've faced my whole life.

I pride myself on my eclectic taste in music, and I've spent enormous portions of time collecting CDs, creating custom mixes, and building my iTunes library. My friends would always say, "Braden, burn me that CD," but I was reluctant. I quickly got a reputation of being a selfish music-hoarder. But was I really to blame—this was my music...those were my secrets, my gems.

Fast forward five years, and every time someone finds some cool music, a cool website, or anything truly unique, they instantly share it with thousands of people. They blog it, they tweet it, and then they publish it on their Facebook feed. And I'm left wondering, "Why?" Certainly I appreciate that we all get to see more cool, unique things whether it be art, music, or even funny local commercials. It's also amazing to see what is essentially a real free market at work—one in which the truly unique and creative ideas emerge.

But does this oversharing destroy the mystique about those best-kept secrets? Doesn't it piss you off when the band that you saw play at your cousin's bar mitzvah is suddenly everyone else's "favorite" band even though they don't know shit about them? Don't you hate it when you can't find that parking space that you thought only you knew about? And don't you hate when that hole-in-the-wall po-boy shop is suddenly the new "it" restaurant?

Cherish your greatest secrets. They are soon to be a thing of the past. 💣

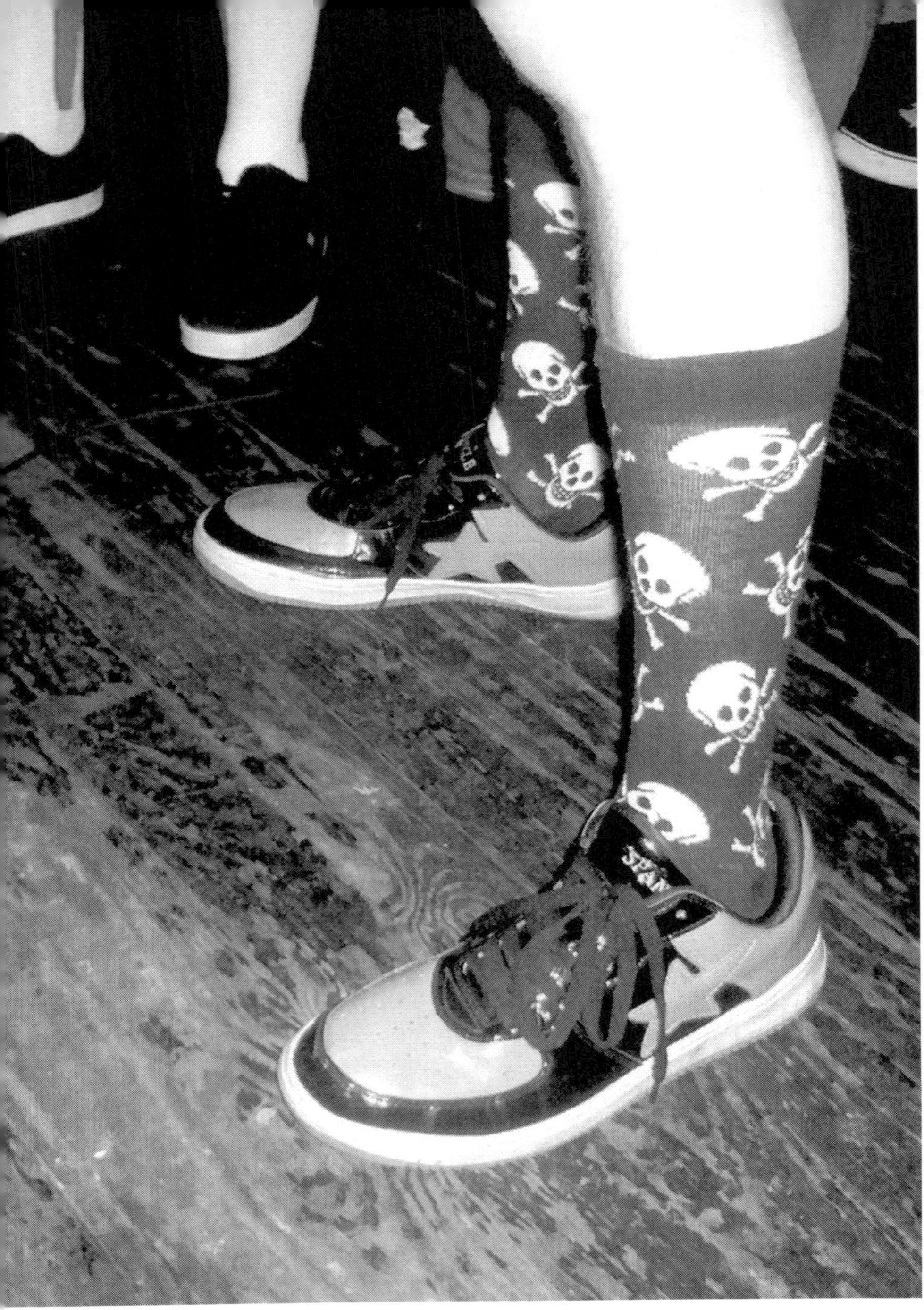

LAST NIGHT THE DJ SAVED MY LIFE

LIZZIE

We all have a secret or two we keep from our friends to maintain that perfect veneer of cool we've been crafting so carefully ever since we discovered ourselves in college. Nothing can lose you cool points like the skeletons in your media closet.

You know what I'm talking about, the stuff that you watch and listen to when no one is around. Behavior so shameful that maybe you hope to take it with you to the grave, like watching Mary-Kate and Ashley films while you're sick, or rooting for one of those delightfully trampy scamps in the "Rock of Love" series (ahem, Daisy), or fueling your insomnia while watching re-runs of "Frasier" on Lifetime at one in the morning. I mean these are just a few random examples of media that you might not be as willing to admit to enjoying as, say, "Mad Men."

However, music is more personal, not just something you enjoy for 30 minutes while flipping channels. Bad music is so much easier to avoid, so when you find yourself downloading "Jagged Little Pill" for "nostalgia," there is no excuse. But there is something about unabashedly loving something I'm supposed to hate that gives me a thrill. Now, "hate" is a strong word, and some might not deem the songs I've picked hate-worthy. But I might be embarrassed to be caught belting them out in the shower or on the subway or something.

BUT THERE IS SOMETHING ABOUT UNABASHEDLY LOVING SOMETHING I'M SUPPOSED TO HATE THAT GIVES ME A THRILL.

OASIS "WONDERWALL"

I can't ever get enough of this song. It seems that without fail it comes on right as that group of drunks in the corner of your favorite bar has reached their peak of rowdiness. One sentimental fellow in the bunch stumbles over to the jukebox and puts this baby on. Let the group hug and sing-along commence.

BRITNEY SPEARS "I'M A SLAVE 4 U"

This is the song that brought me over to the dark side. I had always professed an undying hatred for all things Britney and then I saw this video. I found myself secretly listening to it over and over. It's just so damned catchy, and the video is hot and ridiculous all at once. Brit Brit's whisper voice over a thumping beat expresses her desire to just dance next to that hot guy she has a crush on.

LIL' KIM "NOT TONIGHT"

No musician makes me blush more than Lil' Kim. "Not Tonight," possibly the most perfect ode to muff diving, still sets my cheeks afire and gets me giggling like a seventh grader during sex ed. It's one of my favorite girl anthems because Lil' Kim isn't afraid to tell it like it is when it comes to bedroom shenanigans. She gives us a run down of all the men that have wronged her in the bedroom by not returning the favor... um... orally. 💣

REDEFINING SECRETS

JENÉ LIGGINS

Let's face it. Secrets are a natural part of life. Everyone has them. Whether they're simple or complex, we carry around some part of us that we simply don't want to share with the world. They function as defense mechanisms to keep others outside of our personal boundaries. That's the darker side of secrets; they frequently carry shame or embarrassment. But maybe it's time to redefine the role secrets play in our lives.

I'm an attorney. The word "lawyer" suggests suits, pearls, hair tightly pulled back in some neurotic bun, and an argumentative personality. But, like the tagline from that old MTV "Diary" show, "You think you know, but you have no idea." Society might see the neatly put together attorney, but inside is a free-spirited, tattooed hippie. This flower child loves yoga, the Beatles, and running around barefoot in the rain. This jet-black-dyed, chemically relaxed hair of mine is just as loved when it's washed and wavy, flowing freely in the breeze. My idols are Marvin Gaye and Malcolm X, not Clarence Thomas and Thurgood Marshall. This is the optimistic world of secrets. It's the place in my heart where I can be the Jené I choose to be, instead of J. Jené Liggins, Esq.

Calling the Bay Area of California my second home, I visit as often as possible. Whenever I go, there's one place I have to see every time, the Haight-Ashbury section of San Francisco. The Haight was the center of the hippie movement and home to the Summer of Love in 1967. It was a melting pot of music, consciousness raising, freedom, creative expression, and politics. I take my pilgrimage to the Haight very seriously. Some laugh at the briefcase-carrying lawyer who has the audacity to love this hub of American counterculture, but that hub is where

I feel most at home, not the courtroom. I'd prefer to wear jeans, a Jimi Hendrix t-shirt, and Converse, not a suit. The Hippie Revolution represents one thing to me—freedom. The unadulterated, unrestricted, unabashed ability to live, laugh, love, think, create, and connect.

I cherish the thought of exchanging all the notary seals and case files for flowers and incense. I'd love a mind with an elevated awareness, instead of an elevated knowledge of civil procedure. It's those elements of autonomy, lack of restrictions, and self-determination that drive me. Sure, I look forward to getting my paycheck every other week as much as the next working person. But I enjoy buying those plane tickets to my personal Mecca—The Haight—much more.

There, the secret side of Jené doesn't have to hide anymore. She's not afraid of what people will think when they see her walking around barefoot. She can wear a hoop in one ear and a feather in the other. Simply stated, she can be the Jené that nobody else knows.

It's time to reclaim the true meaning of secrets. They're often assumed to be dangerous or bad. Secrets allow me to have something in my life that's just for me. In this generation of BlackBerries, email, Skype, and myriad other ways to stay connected, it's nice to know there's a place inside that only I have access to. Secrets represent a hidden inner world where we can retreat and hide from the mores of society. So, excuse me while I kiss the sky. 💣

I CHERISH THE THOUGHT OF EXCHANGING ALL THE NOTARY SEALS AND CASE FILES FOR FLOWERS AND INCENSE.

CUBICLE

KAT HARO

Designed in 1968 to provide workers with individual space, room to pin up work in progress, and a way to see work beyond the traditional In Box and Out Box, cubicles were the hottest thing since sliced bread (and, between us, it hadn't been that long). They were going to revolutionize the way modern offices functioned and improve worker productivity beyond belief.

But with the development of this new workspace, did our business forefathers in fact create barriers and enable more efficient gossip machines? Our little boxes were not designed with secrets and hidden gestures in mind, yet they seem so perfectly suited for our modern behaviors.

Water coolers are the proverbial centers for office rumor mongering, but when you have something really juicy to tell, you know you just pop into your work-buddy's cube.

Office friendships are more common than not these days. With the line between personal and work lives blurring with each new social networking platform, it is harder and harder to separate the people who know what account you work on from the people who know what color your spring break bikini was. And for all the arguments for strong personal relationships at work, do you really want them to know everything? And possibly more importantly, do you want to know everything about them? I have coworkers who religiously protect their non-work persona—declining Facebook friendships, blocking their Twitter updates, and using LinkedIn as their sole online connection to the work world. Others bring their weekend to work with them and spend Mondays gathered in the Creative Department joking about not remembering where that bruise came from. I labored over my photo selection, making sure to convey a mixture of laid-back and professional, outdoorsy and modern, friend and animal. My work-mates know about my irrational fear of whales, and my adoration of well organized closets. I'd write what they don't know as well, but then again, what if they read this...

With secrets, as with the rest of life, there is no black/white outline of propriety. Personal preferences and comfort levels weigh in on all of our personal decisions; consequently, our lives inside the cubicle walls may or may not match our lives outside of them.

Walking the office halls you get glimpses of personality perhaps, but you never know what is withheld. The benign collection of family photos, lunch coupons, and calendars that predictably litter most cubicle walls are little indication of the horrors (and wonders) that those cardboard-like structures routinely absorb. I believe the phrase is—if these walls could talk...

Account Director X saunters gleefully down the Account Services hallway, sly smile upon her lips, when suddenly she disappears through an ergonomically correct cube opening and dips below the moderately sized file cabinet for some added privacy as she addresses her colleague in hushed tones. You feel the vibrations of Account Assistant Y's phone and she giggles a little on the other side of the flimsy half wall. All of it makes you wonder—What are my coworkers not telling me? 💣

Image via: http://www.flickr.com/photos/alyssafilmmaker/

SHE.IT. US.THEM.

ASHLEY CHAPMAN

I turn right, going the opposite direction down the one-way street. I secretly wish that a speeding car, blinded by the incessant rain, would hit this sorry excuse for a vehicle. That way I could skip class tomorrow and sleep all day. I would turn the heat up to Hell and laugh as my roommates suffocate.

I reach my house, neglecting the umbrella under my seat, and hope that the rain will disguise my tears. As the water soaks my clothes I begin to cry and laugh. My emotions are everywhere—on my shoulder where my heart is, in my throat where my air is, in my clenched hands.

Before putting the key in my front door, I hear laughter. After I cross the threshold, the laughter ends, and in its place is their silence and my sadness. I look up to find The Three staring at each other.

Totally ignored, I leave water, mud, and tears on the gray tile floor. A strong sudden push on my bladder makes me hurry to the bathroom. I shove my too-small jeans down, but I feel a trickle of warm liquid run down my leg. I rush to

MY SMILE FADES AS I REMEMBER SATURDAY NIGHT... I NEVER HEARD THE DOOR OPEN.

sit on the cold porcelain, knowing that drop of urine will be the most warmth I feel tonight. I throw the pants and panties I just had on into the hamper. I grab the sweatpants hanging on the towel rack and pull them on. Stepping toward the toothpaste-stained sink, I don't want to look at myself in the mirror.

I wash my hands, reach for the cocoa butter, and leave the bathroom never having looked up at the mirror. I know The Three see me as I exit the bathroom. I want them to love me enough to ask. Maybe they are embarrassed. I imitate their emotions as I turn toward my bedroom. I try to avoid the unease.

Sitting on my half-made bed, I stare at the television. It reflects my image, but the picture is dark and blurry.

Looking at my reflection in the TV, I wish I loved myself more. Maybe I wish they loved me enough to accept my love for ones like me, like us.

I lotion my cold dry hands. I lotion my long dark arms covered in cold bumps from the draft rushing from the crack in the window to my left. I lotion my stomach, paying special attention to the cinnamon line that descends beyond my pants. I think of Her. I lotion my cold breasts. I think of Her warmth. I think of Her hands. I smile at my reflection. I hear three laughs.

My smile fades as I remember Saturday night. The Three said they were going to D.C. for the weekend. I invited Her over. We laughed, we ate, and we danced. I turned on D'Angelo. "Nothing Even matters." I never heard the door open. I never heard my name called. All I felt was three stares. I was—like I am now—topless, smelling like cocoa butter, only that time she was beside me. All I felt was their shame.

I turn away from the TV in search of a hoodie. I cover my bare chest. I turn off the lights. I pray for sleep as The Three laugh in the kitchen.

I sleep well. I missed dreaming for many nights after Saturday. I dream tonight though, I dream of light. I wake up to truth and honesty.

It's 10 a.m. and they are in the kitchen already. I breathe in heavily, let it out. I am ready. The sun has warmed up the room. I open the door, walk to the bathroom, and wash my hands. I rinse my mouth and look at myself in the mirror. The image is clear. My flaws and assets are obvious and I can accept them. I want to love myself more but that's going to be a daily task—a lot of shit to work out, but I'm ready.

I walk into the kitchen. They look up, but not at me. I smile and grab a glass of water. The Three are silent as I infringe on the camaraderie of the kitchen space. I ignore the pain of nothingness, turning toward them with acceptance of myself and hope of their acceptance of me.

I sit down next to One. Friends since third grade, we are often mistaken for sisters. Her short thick hair mocks my long brown tresses, but our tall thick bodies are often covered by each other's clothes. I look at the brown shirt she wears and realize it's mine. I remember taking that shirt off my body in front of Her. I wonder how One would feel knowing I wiped Her sweat with it.

Two ends the silence. She laughs, finally some modicum of humanity. She asks me about Him, still avoiding my eye contact. I think of a way to answer.

"Him is not Her. He left and wants to come back. Sometimes I allow him the pleasure of my company but only in denial of hers."

Three coughs nervously. They all look at each other in surprise and disgust. I want to get mad because I feel like The Three don't want to listen. They are not hearing me. I need eye contact to make sure they understand. I look at the glass. Its perspiration reminds me of a slow rain. I push the glass off the smooth brown table. The loud noise finally gets their attention. They look at the glass. The Three look at me as if I'm deranged. I think to myself, "finally." I guess I'm being selfish now. "Look at me," I say not too loudly.

I'm ready. "I'm gay." 💣

THE PARADOX THAT IS FACEBOOK

BRADEN PIPER

I hate Facebook. But I want to be on it. I recently took a hiatus from Facebook because it was making me angry. I found that Facebook was being used more frequently as a tool to market things to me, or to advertise to me, than it was being used as a tool for people to connect with me.

I received anywhere from three to fifteen event invitations a day, and if I happened to put "maybe attending" to any of these events I'd inevitably receive two or three messages from the event creator making sure I didn't forget. Needless to say, I didn't go to any of these events.

In fact, I don't think I've ever gone to an event that I learned about solely through Facebook. I found that the frequency of someone writing on my wall, or commenting on a picture, or sending me a message was so low in comparison to all of the spam I received through Facebook that it wasn't worth it.

So I deactivated my Facebook account. *crowd gasps*

This disturbed quite a few of my peers, as over the next several weeks people kept questioning me with a slight air of confusion, "Did you disable your Facebook account?" "What happened to your Facebook?" "Is something wrong with your Facebook?" as if I had contracted some kind of terrible disease. Sure, people asked me what happened to my Facebook, but they didn't even think to ask how I was. At one point I received an email from a classmate, "I tried to contact you through Facebook, but I guess you don't have an account…"

Why is Facebook the norm for contacting classmates about school matters? I cannot tell you how many times I've heard someone say something like, "If you don't have a Facebook account, then you don't exist."

Stop. Think about that. Think of all the information you have about yourself on Facebook. Think about how easily anyone can access that information. Is Facebook the predecessor to some kind of elaborate government computer filing all humans in an elaborate database where they can sort people by interests, etc.? What if they start predicting the likelihood you'll become a criminal and prosecute you before you even commit a crime? Has anyone seen "Minority Report?"

Ok, so maybe that's a bit of a stretch. But do think about this: For all the "connectivity" Facebook seems to be about, how connected to other people do you really feel? And yet, if you remove yourself from the Facebook world, like I tried, in search of genuine human connection, you'll be hard pressed to find it. Because everyone has gotten so attached to it, they can't imagine life without it. Paradoxically, Facebook is the only thing keeping people connected, but it's systematically destroying their ability to connect with others.

I will not lie; this makes me angry. I've gotten angry before, and I've written about it, and I had only one solution in mind to solve that problem, and the same solution applies here…

Anyone feel like a revolution? 💣

IT'S THE END OF THE WORLD, AS WE KNOW IT

PJ DOSER

The world is coming to an end. What's going to kill us first? If it's not swine flu, it's the collapse of the global economy, or North Korea's testing of nukes, not to mention no one gets their news at the source anymore. When the End of Days comes, you'll probably hear about it on Twitter. But fret not, my friends of the coming apocalypse. Instead, prepare yourself by watching the following films, or at least be entertained by these spot-on views of your futures.

"IT STARTS WITH AN EARTHQUAKE"

"Deep Impact" — Leder, 1998
A comet collides with earth. The only way to survive is to seek refuge in Missouri. The future's pretty grim for everyone, with the exception of a select few; better brush up on your skills so you're necessary. The president is also black in the movie. You put two and two together.

"SAVE YOURSELF, SERVE YOURSELF"

"28 Days Later" — Boyle, 2002
Two Words for you: swine flu. I'm following Biden's advice, in combination with this movie. If you become infected I will kill you to save myself.

"SIX O'CLOCK - TV HOUR. DON'T GET CAUGHT IN FOREIGN TOWER"

"Dr. Strangelove or: How I Learned to Stop Worrying and Love the Bomb" — Kubrick, 1964
Sure, the chances of nuclear holocaust based on a stupid mistake has decreased now that Bush is out of office. But if it happens, fingers crossed it's this funny; and we'll protect our fluids by forgoing water with fluoride. 💣

YOU CAN HAVE WHATEVER YOU WANT. SO LONG AS YOU'RE WILLING TO FOCUS ON MAKING IT HAPPEN... INDEFINITELY.

MORAL OF THE DAY

ALBUM REVIEW: AUTOLUX "TRANSIT TRANSIT"

ALEX PALUMBO-GREEN

Los Angeles rock trio Autolux, comprising of bassist Eugene Goreshter, drummer Carla Azar, and guitarist Greg Edwards, step back into view with their sophomore album, "Transit Transit."

The album dropped in early August and comes as a long-anticipated offering after their premiere 2004 album, "Future Perfect." A lot of the best aspects of "Future Perfect" are still here on "Transit Transit." However, like a lot of sophomore efforts, there's experimentation that doesn't always pay off.

"Future Perfect" presented a surfeit of sound for a three-piece band. Brilliant and imaginative pop songs coupled melancholy with vivid and borderline nonsensical lyrics. Dirty and distorted bass tones played against guitar riffs that jumped between bright, warm tones and fuzzed-out feedback; all backed by ass-kicking krautrock-esque beats.

> IT'S BEEN SIX YEARS SINCE AUTOLUX'S FIRST ALBUM, AND THEY'RE STILL JUST AS GOOD AS THEY WERE THEN.

All of that is on "Transit Transit" as well. Tracks like "Census," "Supertoys," "Audience No. 2," and "Kissproof" are written and predominantly sung by Eugene, and maintain the established Autolux sound. As such, these songs are the most endearing and probably the best songs on the album. They share a significant similarity with songs from the first album. The beat for "Audience No. 2" is damn similar to "Future Perfect" opener "Turnstile Blues." Allusions to the first album are made throughout and serve as distinguished reminders of their past effort, such as during the chorus to "Supertoys," when Carla sings, "It's alright. You're okay. It's in your future broken."

There are, however, parts of "Transit Transit" where new ideas are introduced and experimented with, but ultimately fall flat. Unfortunately, these parts belong to the songs written by Greg. It's noticeably his first time taking a more proactive role in songwriting and it's radically different. While there is nothing wrong with Greg's lyrical writing, the musical aspects of his songs are rather lacking. We first observe this with the self-titled album opener, "Transit Transit." It's a complete departure from past Autolux. There's a ticking drum machine accompanied by piano balladry and floating synthesizer ambience. Similar problems repeat themselves on Greg-written tracks

"High Chair" and "Spots." It all sounds less like Autolux and more like abandoned tracks from the "Kid A" and "Amnesiac" days of Radiohead.

This is not to say experimentation doesn't pay off for Autolux. The sixth track, "The Bouncing Wall," is a Carla-written and sung song featuring her lovely and soft vocal styling, coupled with her excellent drumming. Greg's guitar work loops in the background and also skips in the forefront by taking full advantage of the recording studio. Eugene's bass is fuzzed out to the point that it sounds like a distorted synth bass. At the same time, Azar's vocals multiply and give the track a satisfying amount of buildup and heft.

The second to last track, "Headless Sky," is written by Eugene and has a darker tone to it. It features a somewhat monotonous looped guitar riff throughout, with Carla's drumming and Eugene's bass coming in after the first half of the song, along with lead guitar noise by Greg, giving the songs a good amount of sonic depth.

The biggest surprise of what the new Autolux has to offer comes in the form of the last track, "The Science of Imaginary Solutions." Here we have a modest beginning, with Azar singing in her usual manner, a light and melodic guitar ringing throughout. Suddenly, both the bass and guitar come crashing over our head with Carla's cymbals. This structure repeats until all members are playing at the same time together. There's a good mix of Greg piano and guitar playing, Carla's drumming and singing, and Eugene's sharp-edged bass. It's the most dynamic song on the album and combines the totality of old and new Autolux together.

All in all, "Transit Transit" is an enjoyable listen. It's been six years since Autolux's first album, and they're still just as good as they were then. "Transit Transit" possesses a lot of the visceral noise rock and melodic pop elements that made "Future Perfect" such a compelling album. It's natural, of course, for a band to want to take risks and try new things as they grow as musicians. While some of the risks taken on "Transit Transit" fail to really flourish into anything worth listening to, there are other risks that prove that Autolux can still deliver the goods. 💣

INTERVIEW: BLAIR

MCCLAIN JOHNSON

Blair is a singer-songwriter born and raised in New Orleans. She is currently based out of Brooklyn, New York. Her debut album, "Die Young," drops January 26 on Autumn Tone Records.

INVADENOLA: YOUR NEW ALBUM IS "DIE YOUNG." HOW DID THE RECORDING PROCESS GO?

Blair: It was kind of a mix. I had some songs that I had written. I released an EP, and I had some songs that I didn't record for the EP. In the two years after the EP, I had some songs floating around. So, basically had three years of songs floating around. Basically, those songs that were floating around are half the record, and then the other half I wrote in about one month when I was out in California for a little while. It's kind of a mix of building up a library of songs, and inspiration striking and writing a bunch more.

That's how the songs came about. I demoed them on GarageBand and worked them out over the years. I got to learn different things with different players. And I went to New Orleans, I had Keith Ferguson and my bandmate, Adam. We were kind of like a creative triangle, and bounced off each other as far as the production went. I recorded it almost two years ago in New Orleans.

IN: YOU'RE LIVING IN BROOKLYN NOW. DO YOU MISS THE SCENE IN NEW ORLEANS?

B: Yeah. I miss New Orleans definitely living-wise, because Brooklyn is probably the complete opposite. It's super crowded, everything is super fast. People don't have time to look you in the eye, much less strike up a conversation. New Orleans is very different. I miss the venues. I miss playing the Circle Bar, the Saturn Bar, and all my friends would come to the show. I definitely miss that, and the weather. I miss all that stuff.

IN: DO YOU FEEL THAT NEW ORLEANS HAS A DIFFERENT SORT OF COMMUNITY THAN BROOKLYN IN TERMS OF THE SCENE?

B: I guess, there are so many more people in Brooklyn. There are so many bands. Take as many bands as there are in New Orleans and multiply it by five hundred. I liked playing with Rotary Downs a lot, and the World Leader Pretend guys are my friends. I guess you could consider that the scene in New Orleans. I felt, with those two bands, there's some camaraderie there. I've almost been here a year. I can say that I have some bands that I like, we're friends, but it's more competitive here. People are really competing, whereas in New Orleans, you feel like you have just a bunch of friends playing. I like some things about both of them.

IN: DID YOU RECORD THIS ALBUM COMPLETELY IN NOLA?

B: Yeah, I did. Like I said, I demoed it just myself, just with a computer, out in California. I came back, and it was the summer of '08. I rented some gear, and got Keith and Adam involved. We'd set up gear in different apartments. Sometimes, the gear would fail, and we'd have to move apartments. It was very DIY, and it was recorded in the span of two and a half months. Some of it was done in my manager's house in Mid-City, and some of it was done out in the Bywater, near Vaughan's.

> NEW ORLEANS IS VERY DIFFERENT. I MISS THE VENUES. I MISS PLAYING THE CIRCLE BAR, THE SATURN BAR, AND ALL MY FRIENDS WOULD COME TO THE SHOW.

IN: WHAT DO YOU FEEL IS THE BIGGEST MISCONCEPTION ABOUT THE SCENE IN NEW ORLEANS?

B: What I found when I was playing there, there's a value for jazz and funk, which I think is important, because it's part of the history of New Orleans. I think there are a lot of other kinds of music there too, whether it be rock and pop, or other stuff that I don't listen to, but I know it's there. People are actively working and trying to let something natural happen. It doesn't have to have a label. It doesn't have to be indie, it doesn't have to be rock, it doesn't have to be pop. It doesn't have to be so packaged. I think, eventually, stuff like that will leak out. If the New Orleans press can give at least half the press that they give to the older names, that have already had 60-year careers, then that would be a good thing.

IN: DO YOU REMEMBER YOUR FIRST GIG IN NOLA?

B: Yeah. My first real gig, I was in high school, and I played an open mic at the Neutral Ground coffeehouse, over in Uptown.

IN: IT DOES SEEM THAT, ESPECIALLY NATIONALLY, PEOPLE DON'T KNOW ABOUT THE INDIE SCENE THAT'S GOING ON IN NEW ORLEANS.

B: Yeah. I think the more that people play and do original shit. Also, just work to reach outside of New Orleans and get people interested in you, then New Orleans itself will have to value all the talent it has in the new genres I'm talking about.

IN: YOU'VE REALLY BEEN ABLE TO MAKE A NAME FOR YOURSELF BY GOING OUT OF NOLA AND TRYING NEW STUFF.

B: Yeah, that's the path I took. It also fit naturally. New Orleans is my hometown, so I was also at a point where I wanted to see other things too. My music is the most important thing to me. Where I moved coincided with being a good place to play pop music. When I got press for that EP, I got the most press in New York and L.A. I might have gotten one article in New Orleans. I was just looking at it like, I should go play where people are going to talk about it. That's what I did.

IN: YOU WENT TO WHERE YOU THOUGHT A GOOD AUDIENCE WOULD BE FOR YOUR SOUND?

B: Yeah, exactly. Geographical scenes are diminishing a little bit because now scenes are online. There are scenes on blogs. It's almost like the city and state is not as relevant as they used to be. I think New Orleans is my favorite place to play. The Saturn Bar is one of my favorite places to play ever. As far as feeling some kind of momentum, I definitely felt it in L.A. and here in Brooklyn more.

IN: I LOVE YOUR FIRST TWO EPS, AND I THINK THIS ALBUM IS GOING TO BE BIG. DO YOU FEEL THAT SORT OF MOMENTUM BEHIND IT?

B: I'm really proud of it. I know it's the best thing I could have written at the time I wrote it. It's the best thing that I could put out there. It has pieces of myself. It does feel special. I just want to quit my day job. That's the first thing, that happens and it's all been worth it. 💣

For more info on Blair, please check out myspace.com/musicblair

ACCESSORIZING POLITICALLY.

TASLIM VAN HATTUM

kaffiyah [kuh-fee-uh]
–noun
an Arab headdress for men; made from a diagonally folded square of cloth held in place by an agal wound around the head.

In 2010, I am leaving myself wrapped up in a fading fad of 2009. Comfortable having people think I am trapped unintentionally in last year's fashion choices, I continue to rock a kaffiyah on any day where there is a chill in the air, and most any night when I simply want an accessory that makes my fashion identity feel complete.

The year 2009 was branded as the "the year of the kaffiyah." Every fashionista and hipster sported the checkered black and white scarves—a scarf that I had been verbally accosted for wearing from September 11, 2001, up until the current hipster trend of 2009. In 2001, I went from being a 2,000-year-old Arab farmer working my olive groves in this scarf to a straight jihadi terrorist hell-bent on Western destruction. On to 2009, when suddenly I was deemed a hip and fashion-forward individual who dressed with effortlessly draped chic.

Earlier in the year, I realized this trend had really taken off when a skinny-jean-clad young man approached me one night and, while covetously fingering the kaffiyah around my neck, asked, "Ohhh where did you get that 'Riviera' scarf?"

(as it had been newly re-named by Urban Outfitters). Who wouldn't rather imagine wrapping oneself in the Riviera-esque bliss of St. Tropez, instead of the war-torn streets of Palestine? Never had a better marketing name change been made than from the unpronounceable and un-relatable "kaffiyah" to "Riviera." I also knew that my honest answer,

the streets. Yet as the year progressed, and they went from black and white to fluorescent, and then to paisley patterned with skulls available in London's Topshop, I started wondering about the greater meanings behind the co-opting of this scarf.

Despite the mainstream media controversy dubbing the kaffiyah

I REALIZED THAT AS MUCH AS I LOVED THE FAMILIARITY OF THE SYMBOL NOW HITTING THE AMERICAN STREETS, DEEP DOWN I HARBORED SADNESS...

"the dirty back alleyway of a Middle Eastern market where I haggled for an hour over a 30-cent price difference," was not the appropriate response. And so I opted for the easier-to-understand "Urban Outfitters, of course."

In the beginning, I was delighted by the popular co-opting of the kaffiyah. I looked around and everyone was wearing them. My first instinct, as someone raised with the cultural and political symbol of the kaffiyah, was delight at seeing their familiarity fill

"hate couture," Rachael Ray's public apology for wearing a kaffiyah on TV, and Dunkin' Donuts being politicized for something other then cream filling, the new "Riviera" scarf was an instant fashion hit! Rappers like Kanye West and celebrities like Sienna Miller draped themselves in it, along with Busta Rhymes in his now infamously insulting "Arab Money" music video, which caused worldwide controversy, resulting in the song's being banned from radio play throughout Europe and the Middle East.

I realized that as much as I loved the familiarity of the symbol now hitting the American streets, deep down I harbored sadness that unlike your average fashionista, I had to make sure not to wear it when traveling. This was the case even as I flew through New Orleans, New York, and Chicago. I saw other young people cozily wrapped in their kaffiyahs without fear of repercussion or assumption.

It was a simple fashion choice on their parts. On me, the kaffiyah wasn't just a fashion accessory, but a conscious historic and political choice of self-representation. It was like kente cloth: on a European, simply being a pretty and colorful design; but on a Ghanian, denoting far more specific connotations about history, tribe, class and class-consciousness.

Although most people in New Orleans might have just fashion-trended their way into kaffiyah-draped hipsterdom, I spent the latter part of 2009 thinking about who this co-opting affected, as well as my own guilt at knowing that I slipped easily into the "I bought it at Urban Outfitters" lie in order to not have to go into depth on a nightclub floor about what a kaffiyah really means and who it represents. These thoughts and emotions led me from just being a fashion follower (which I will admit gave me a superiority complex borne out of knowing the true meaning of the garment, and therefore feeling as though I knew oh-so-much more then these average hipsters wearing it) to joining others in action surrounding the kaffiyah. While it was great to see so many people wearing kaffiyahs, it meant little if they didn't know what they were wearing, and so 2009 seemed like the time to not only wear a kaffiyah, but also to help others wearing it learn something more about it.

In response to the exploding fashion trend, a group of New Orleanians launched the Kufiyeh Project (thekufiyehproject.org), a project seeking to explore and support the historical and cultural significance of the kaffiyah and share it with the larger public. The project seeks to promote ethical purchasing of the kaffiyah from original sources to promote indigenous industry as a means of cultural preservation. Locating the last remaining

IF I AM WEARING KAFFIYAH IN 2010, I WANT MORE THAN IMITATION ON A MASS-PRODUCED AND MEANINGLESS SCALE.

original kaffiyah factory in Hebron, whose business has been decimated by cheap mass-produced Chinese imports, the project set up direct marketing systems, with original scarves being sold at a mere $12, cheaper by almost $13 than Urban Outfitters scarves, and supporting the actual people who they represent.

This fashion trend of 2009, although now fading out with most people none the wiser about the politics of the accessory (a fault of my own when I did not take the time to educate kaffiyah-coveters further when approached), continues to remind me about my own purchasing practices particularly as I approach the new year ready for fresh, intentional and conscious starts.

If I am wearing kaffiyah in 2010, I want more than imitation on a mass-produced and meaningless scale. I want clothing and accessories that are representative and contribute to my community, not a ripped-off accessory that appears trendy but has no relation to my own culture, and identity.

I can't say I am sad to see my chosen accessory's popularity fade into last year's fashion history. My feelings about its rise to meteoric popularity are complex, both happy and sad, but I rest assured knowing that like with any fashion fad, it is sure to be reborn again, recycled and renamed sometime again in the future. And when it does I will remind myself that regardless of its branded name this time around, I am responsible for explaining to others honestly what a kaffiyah represents, whose factory they should be purchasing it from, and that it means more then just being stylish and warm. 💣

WHEN SOMEONE PISSES YOU OFF, QUIETLY SAY TO YOURSELF, "FUCK YOU VERY MUCH" AND THEN LET IT GO.

NO NEED HOLDING A GRUDGE.

MORAL OF THE DAY

GROWN-UPS DON'T LET GROWN UPS PASS ON STDS

KAREN ALISE

A couple of weeks ago, my best friend caught chlamydia. Actually, a couple weeks ago my best friend discovered that she had caught chlamydia somewhere within the six-month period between her regular tests, but she had no idea from whom it came.

She had gone to the clinic that day like any promiscuous, yet healthy, adult, with the confident belief that her genitalia were uninfected and the desire to simply be proven right.

"Any symptoms?" the nurse asked.

"No. This is just my regular six-month checkup," she answered back proudly, with a smile. She always practiced safe sex, and whenever she left a clinic, she was never ashamed to take a handful of free condoms. When the procedure was finished, they told her she did not have AIDS, and that if she had any other infections, they would call her. She sauntered out of the clinic and decided that tonight, she would have sex just to celebrate.

A couple days later, she got that phone call. One of her whores had passed on chlamydia. It was probably the one who brought one condom and then slipped it off when she wasn't looking, or it could have been the guy with whom the condom had popped. His massive slab of manhood was far too big for her normal-size Trojans. It was either one of those two, or it was her regular booty call. She had so many grown-up sleepovers with him that he had boyfriend privileges with condoms; however, seeing as neither of them were monogamous, his right to go raw should definitely have been revoked.

"Make sure you tell your partner," the nurse instructed, but that statement was a slap in the face. For the past six months, she had multiple orgasms with multiple partners.

She was treated and didn't have sex for a whole two weeks, just to be sure it had cleared from her system. Her health was restored, but this next step was toying with her dignity. The past six months' partners all thought they were in bed with a Snow White type, not a Jezebel. Besides, in her tiny college community, news spreads faster than a cold in a pre-school. She wasn't ready to be known as a dirty whore. However, the preacher's daughter moralist in her knew that it was her responsibility to tell her partners to all get tested.

We devised a plan to tell these boys anonymously. We sent a text to the first guy from my phone number: "U gave me chlamydia. Handle that." He called, and she ignored it, then we texted back. Keeping it anonymous: "just go handle it." He asked who it was, but she refused to identify herself. That was it, bachelor number one was in the know.

The next guy didn't have a cell phone when she met him at a house party, but she hadn't anticipated seeing him ever again. She did, of course, have him as a friend on Facebook. It's moments like these that the honesty box was invented for. For those

OUR DEVICES WERE PRETTY IMMATURE, BUT SHE HAD DONE HER GROWN UP DUTY.

who are too cool for Facebook, the honesty box feature allows you to send a message to someone anonymously. Our message was, "I may have given you chlamydia." His response was, "Who the fuck is this?" My girl answered, "just get tested."

The third guy had been the worst sexual experience of her life, and part of her didn't want to tell him at all. But the thought that some unsuspecting woman would be the victim of both bad sex and an STD was more than this preacher's daughter could handle. She didn't have his phone number either, she'd tossed his business card out soon as she left his house. All she had on him was a URL to his blog site. So she logged in and left an anonymous comment that read, "Hey, I may have given you chlamydia. I wouldn't have told you so publicly, but I lost your phone number. Get tested." She was satisfied by the knowledge that she had both informed him and gotten him back for a horrible night.

Our devices were pretty immature, but she had done her grown-up duty. I assume that without the exhaustive use of technology, she probably wouldn't have told any of these guys. And it's not just getting tested regularly, but it's also informing your past partners that will keep STDs from spoiling all our grown-up fun. Remember to get tested regularly, and tell your partner(s) when your body isn't 100 percent Snow White pure. It's the adult thing to do. 💣

Image via: http://www.flickr.com/photos/44442915@N00/

PEE AFTER SEX

KAREN ALISE

I woke up a cold, late December morning to a sore back and hips. My body had been the victim of my sexual appetite for past couple of days, and it seemed that nothing could stop me from pretty much nagging my boyfriend into making sexy with me.

Thankfully his bathroom was about three feet from his bed, so it was only a matter of rolling myself to the foot of his California King and shyly venturing a warm foot onto cold tile to get to the toilet. My nude body tensed and awoke when it made contact with a frozen white toilet seat. But I relaxed and let it flow until Shit Mother Fucker Shit! It felt like I was trying to pass a burning match through my vagina.

I knew—more like hoped—that it was not an STD, because my boyfriend and I get tested together, so unless he was a slick bastard, it was some other problem. I decided to turn to the ever-faithful Google for the answer to my burning query. Turns out, I had a urinary tract infection. Although anyone can get this infection, it is most commonly found in sexually active women. Crikey. I've never been pregnant or had an STD, but the sex gods still managed to get me.

As I am not big on doctors, cold hands, or hospitals, I decided to continue searching the web for home remedies for my situation. The answer was cranberry juice and more water. My mom has been telling me about the wonders of cranberry juice since that first ride along the crimson tide, yet apparently I hadn't gotten the message. I had the boyfriend take me to the nearest grocery store so I could get myself some cranberry juice. I got the super organic unsweetened stuff in a glass bottle from a bog in Vermont, just to be certain that I got the full cranberry effect. Who knew that cranberries in their purest form were more pungent than biting into pickled limes?

I kept on the cranberry juice and water regimen, which only meant that I was peeing at an accelerated rate. And the more I peed, the more tears I shed. The next morning I woke up and it felt like my stomach was being used to tether a ship. It wasn't a woman-time pain, it was far worse. From then on, I began to contemplate suicide. I figured that I needed to take that cranberry juice more seriously. I drank more juice, I braved the sting of my pee, but the pain only seemed to worsen. It was definitely time to go to the hospital, but not until after Christmas.

I stomached two ibuprofen, got as sexy as one can be in flat shoes, and went to the Christmas Eve party that my best friend was throwing. I felt like a diabetic at Willy Wonka's watching the overflow of an open bar in which

AS I AM NOT BIG ON DOCTORS, COLD HANDS, OR HOSPITAL'S, I DECIDED TO CONTINUE SEARCHING THE WEB FOR HOME REMEDIES FOR MY SITUATION.

I could not participate. I asked the bartender for a cranberry juice and imagined the taste of Grey Goose vodka. Moreover, I could barely hold a conversation because it seemed that with every complicated thought came the desire to pee. I asked around for another ibuprofen. In a room full of women, there will always be at least one walking pharmacy. I thanked her with every frail bone in my body.

"Cramps?" she asked as she handed me my pills.

"No, I have a UTI," I answered back, almost hoping that she was my fairy godmother and that she would save me.

"Well, do you pee after sex?"

I wanted to answer, "Eventually." How am I supposed to remember each time I pee?

She seemed to fathom my hesitation, because she said, "Girl, if you can't shower immediately after sex, then make sure you pee."

As soon as she said it, I was like "Duh!" I'm no nurse or anything, and the thought of anything scientific makes me want to cry, but it's so obvious. Your urine washes away that nasty boy-bacteria that you collect on your flower during sex. Why had no one told me before, I wondered. I was doubled over in pain and unable to drink on Christmas Eve, and the solution was as simple as taking a slightly inconvenient piss. I took the ibuprofen and felt deceptively better. I even drank a little... a lot. I had to catch up on the drinks that I missed in addition to taking advantage of the fact that the bar was more open than a hooker on crack after she'd made her nightly quota.

I woke up on Christmas morning feeling like Santa had run out of coal and discovered a much worse punishment. I was in more pain than before, thanks to my good judgment the night before. I just had to make it through my dad's Christmas breakfast and then I could hit that ER. In my father's eyes, I am still a virgin, so I made no mention of my illness and thanked him and his wife graciously when he handed me my gift.

I was the first to dash off. I took a cab to the hospital, where I was one of only a few people. There was a boy who had slipped on some ice and a baby with an ear infection, but apparently sick people don't go to the hospital on Christmas Day. In the examination room, I was told that my UTI had progressed to a severe infection, and I almost laughed. Guess all that cranberry juice didn't do much. I swallowed the first installment of my prescription and from then on I vowed to be the voice behind the movement, telling women to pee after sex. 💣

WHEN YOU LOOK BACK ON YOUR LIFE IS THIS THE MEMORY YOU WANT OF YOUR TWENTIES.

MORAL OF THE DAY

Image via: http://www.flickr.com/photos/bfsminid/

BROKE-ASS HOMEOWNER: DECOR ON A BUDGET

SARAH ANDERT

One year ago, I bought a newly renovated house in Holy Cross with seven rooms' worth of blank space: 1,400 square feet and 14-foot ceilings. Since I was broke enough to get the government to pay for half my mortgage, I wondered how I'd ever have the money to decorate it like a "real" home.

Goodbye crumbling slum-lord plaster and water-stained rental shitrock; hello smooth-as-a-baby's-ass, glossy fresh walls—this was my chance! After months of stockpiling magazines from *Bust* to *Architectural Digest* I had plenty of ideas, but my house still looked like a stark corporate rental. I realized that making my home legit yet cozy, and personal but not haphazard, on a budget of zero, was going to take some creativity—creativity, I eventually discovered, that didn't even need to come from me.

Allow me to present three bold new ways to decorate your house yourself in the New Year.

DATE AN ARTIST.

These people are constantly doodling, snapping photos, making collages, and generally leaving things lying around. They tend to be messy and easily distracted, so pilfering a few sketches or "work prints" to frame at home shouldn't be too difficult. If you're young and single, date around. You never know who's going to be worth something in a few decades. Or if you're willing to invest more time in the relationship, it's pretty safe to assume you'll receive an original work of art for your birthday or a holiday. I'd also suggest attending the gallery opening of a friend of your significant other and hinting that you'd love it if they traded pieces as a gift for your next birthday. This should expand your collection without any additional allocation of resources on your part.

MAKE A PILGRIMAGE TO PONCHATOULA.

I love a good vintage find, and "Mad Men" makes the 1960s look hot. It's rewarding to successfully combine antiques, mid-century modern and contemporary décor in a way that suits my tastes. But in a city that so totally fetishizes old shit, I find it nearly impossible to get a good deal on secondhand clothing, furniture, and household wares in New Orleans. Is it because the good stuff got washed away? Because we're all too broke to sell anything at a reasonable price? Or because there's no morally righteous, solid middle class to recycle items to charity? In answer to my dilemma, I recently discovered that Ponchatoula sells a lot more than strawberries; apparently it's "America's Antique City." Some of its stores were unimpressive, but one stood apart—C.J.'s Antiques and Collectibles, the mother of all junk shops. It was so big that I got lost. I spent two hours in there. My sister had to go outside for fresh air because she grew faint from all the sorting, sifting, and squinting at jumbled, dusty objects for sale. I spent 15 bucks and came home with three 1940s prints I will "creatively" hang in mismatched dollar frames from the Green Project, and three little catchpenny paintings that will make a nice arrangement on my bedroom wall.

JOIN THE WIN/WIN NOLA BARTERING NETWORK.

Currency is just another way for the man to keep his foot on your neck, right? Join WIN/WIN and never feel nickled-and-dimed again. This network of local folks hooks up via Facebook to trade goods and services, including works of art and other crafts, cash free. And tax free, so long as you're not dumb enough to report something like that on your income tax return. Of course, this means you'll need to share whatever you have in order to get what you need, but I'm sure you'll think of something. 💣

INTERVIEW: BIONICA

LAURA KLEIN

What do you get when you combine jazz, funk, electronica, happiness, and insanity? Pretty much Bionica. This young New Orleans band melds multiple genres per song and gives off an intoxicating energy that makes you feel lovely just because you're a part of it.

The talent consists of keyboardist/ vocalist Rex Gregory, vocalist/ keyboardist Sasha Masakowski, bassist Devin Kerrigan, drummer/ percussionist Nick Solnick, and vocalist/keytarist/"unofficial band leader" James Westfall. Bionica's first EP drops this month, so now is the time to jump on the band's wagon. InvadeNOLA's got your back, giving you the inside scoop straight from Bionica.

INVADENOLA: SO HOW DID YOU GUYS GET TOGETHER?
Sasha: Well it was originally James's band, but then it was called Bionic Dream. We decided to change the name to Bionica when [we] came up with an idea for women's clothing.
Nick: Sasha, Rex, and I met in Holland during the [Hurricane] Katrina evacuation. We froze our asses off and made beautiful music, and James and Rex had met each other back in Houston, and we started with a different bassist [before Devin]. But we've all been playing together for a little over a year now.
Devin: Yeah, I had a pretty intense audition process. Basically I had to learn the songs and then play them at the show that night. But it was a kickass show. I guess it wasn't that hard.

Rex: James was the unofficial leader, he wrote the first songs. We kept doing music and played steadily, and we just recorded our first EP.
Nick: Yeah, it's been pretty quick.
Rex: Quick and cool.

IN: WHAT'S THE SIGNIFICANCE OF THE NAME BIONICA?
Sasha: It sort of suggests robotic.
Rex: The name means applying processes in life to machines; trying to find the life in the machine, or for the machine.

IN: HOW WOULD YOU DESCRIBE YOUR MUSIC?
Nick: It's a little electronic. When you get all that jazz music with a bunch of electronic keyboardists and tell them to write rock music, this is what you get. Like Miles Davis said about Wayne Shorter: "He doesn't need to do anymore because it's all already there."
Devin: Dude, you stole that quote from my presentation.
Nick: I did. And now I'm applying it to Bionica.
Rex: Bionica, it's all there.

IN: YOU GUYS HAVE SOME INDIVIDUAL SIDE PROJECTS AS WELL?
Sasha: I have a few other side projects: Nova Nola, Brazil Jazz Group, Musical Playground and the Cliff Hines Quintet, which James also plays in.
Rex: Yeah, everyone plays with everyone.
Nick: Yeah, Devin and I play together with other bands; I play in like five or six other bands, but Bionica is the band I'm most passionate about. We're all independent, we're working musicians. We take what we learn [separately] and build from that collectively.
Sasha: And we all have sex with Devin.
Rex: Yeah.
Nick: Devin is the slut of the group. Your browser may not support display of this image.

IN: WHAT'S ONE OF YOUR FAVORITE PLACES TO PLAY GIGS AROUND HERE?
Nick: One Eyed Jack's, they have great sound.
Rex: They hook it up.
Sasha: Yeah, that place has a really good vibe, the people appreciate us, and they appreciate the music.

WE'RE ALL INDEPENDENT. WE'RE WORKING MUSICIANS. WE TAKE WHAT WE LEARN [SEPARATELY] AND BUILD FROM THAT

IN: WHAT WOULD YOU SAY IS YOUR BIGGEST COLLECTIVE STRENGTH?
Nick: The fact that there's so much talent in the musicians of the band.
Devin: Even when we're struggling to hear each other we still try hard to... hear each other?
Sasha: Devin's sex appeal.
Rex and Nick: Yes.
Sasha: We all have very strong opinions; we're political and philosophical people, and these aren't just sappy love songs.
Rex: Main strength: Purpose.

IN: OKAY, YOU'RE ALL HANGING OFF A CLIFF, AND SOME RANDOM GUY SAYS HE WILL ONLY SAVE ONE OF YOU, AND YOU GUYS HAVE TO AGREE ON WHO HE SAVES. SO WHO GETS TO LIVE AND WHY?

Rex: Maybe Sasha, because robots can play keyboards, but they can't sing.
Devin: I already fell.
Nick: I was gonna say Devin so he could go on to spread his seed and create little Bionicans.
Sasha: Yeah!
Devin: Oh well, I'm already saved then... Y'all just want me to live with the guilt.

IN: CAN YOU TELL ME ABOUT THIS EP? AND THE DETAILS OF YOUR NEAREST SHOWS?

Sasha: The EP is entitled "Take Your City," which is also one of the tracks.
Nick: ...And "Take Your City" is about taking our city back, right?
Rex: It's about the people with all the power having broken all their promises, so we're taking [the power] back.
Sasha: Another song, "Our Town," is about an old man who gets no respect and finally becomes sick of it, and he goes on a massive killing spree.
Rex: Another one ["Commodore"] is really energetic, and also very tense. [The Commodore] was the first personal computer. 💣

For more information about Bionica or upcoming shows, check them out:

bionicaband.com
myspace.com/bionicaband
facebook.com/bionicaband

Image via: http://www.flickr.com/photos/71078118@N00/2102264370/

DEAR HIPSTER MALE

JUSTIN SHIELS

Or perhaps I should call you a metrosexual. Yes, I know the term was coined in the early 2000s, but the effects of the trend have had permanent ramifications on our hypermaterialistic society.

I see you over there with your skinny ties and grandpa sweaters.

I've noticed your dark skinny jeans and your faux tap shoes.

And even when you've worn red flannel, it was not to chop wood or do work outdoors. Instead it was to sip Old Fashioneds in some dive bar in the Marigny.

But here's the thing: fuck old America's constructs of masculinity. It is perfectly acceptable to harness your personal brand. You've got money to spend and you're living in a modern day Metropolis (or at least in Mid-City New Orleans). Embrace your affinity for color-coordinated ensembles. Buy that new pair of Supras. And most of all, demand that your girlfriend step it up a notch... to at least match your new swag. 💣

Image via: Lizzie Ford-Madrid
http://lizziefordmadrid.com

FAT IN THIN TIMES

KAREN ALISE

General Motors collapsed in 2009 after 101 years of being the symbol of our highly industrialized nation. And entire industries were begging Obama for a bailout, but have Chanel or Hermès even so much as slashed their prices since the economy dipped?

Have you ever heard of a liquor store going out of business? Have you managed to stop smoking despite the rising prices of cigarettes? "I think not," answered my wallet. The fact is, some industries are just plain recession proof. That is because when times are hard, instead of completely saving our pennies, we use a trip to the store to reward ourselves for frugality. Oh, don't pretend like I'm the only one who refuses to cut the fat in these terribly thin times.

I've been eating leftovers for the past couple of weeks, which actually means the same box of cereal I ate for breakfast is what I ate for dinner the preceding night. But I've got a pair of blue suede pumps arriving via UPS that I ordered online. Here's hoping that my account doesn't overdraft. Folks, we are living in thin times, but that doesn't mean we've managed to cut down on our vices, now we're just now using them as therapy as we weather the storm. So those blue pumps that I bought are not a slice of luxury, they are actually self-prescribed medication.

So in order for us to keep up with our necessary vices, I've compiled a short list of ways to save money in these uncertain times.

BUY CHEAP ALCOHOL

Sure, the good stuff goes down more smoothly, and people with class and money will be able to smell it on your breath, but what does all that matter when you are happily oblivious to all social code on only $15 a handle?

SHOP CONSIGNMENT SHOPS

I know it feels like a fall from grace to leave with a pre-owned Chanel purse, especially if that purse is not in a Chanel paper shopping bag but in a plastic bag with the face of a dog on it. However, you can throw together some really cool outfits that supersede trendy and move into a realm of really cool. I especially love the fact that there is a guarantee that no one else will be cramping my style on the streets. Besides, the stuff in consignment shops is usually close to brand new, so only you can tell that you've bought an iguana-skin purse for one-fifteenth of the original price.

GET TO THE CLUB EARLY

Who are we trying to impress? Get to the club early while it's still free and relax. Wait till all the cool kids roll in, and then pretend to yourself that you arrived only moments before they did. No one will be the wiser, except fellow early birds. Your feet may be tired by the end of the night, and you may have been there long enough to hear some of the hits played twice, but if you pre-game with cheap alcohol none of those things will really matter.

ENFORCE CHIVALRY

There was a time when I fancied myself a feminist, but I have since learned that I am not ready to let go of the expectation that the guy will pay for everything, and neither should you. I've since decided, and I hope you join me, to quit trying to make the world a better place and allow myself to be cosseted and cradled in the security of a world where a woman's responsibility does not extend beyond the beauty of her toes.

GO TO THE DOLLAR STORE

No, I am not suggesting you buy random brands of things, but what you may not know is that dollar stores have name-brand items. They have Colgate toothpaste and Reynolds aluminum foil and, my favorite, Garnier Fructis hair products. I like to hit the dollar store before going to a major chain for the best possible deals. Only better deal is to buy these things off a man selling them from a duffle bag on the corner.

In conclusion, cut the costs where you can to allow more things you absolutely love. Those things may include much of the food pyramid or going anywhere that isn't free before 11, but eventually the shoes, cigs, and alcohol will numb you to the pain of the recession. 💣

BLOGGING IS DEAD

JUSTIN SHIELS

And anyone who believes it's alive has been tricked by the trendiest zombie infecting the interwebs.

It was 2003. I was a senior in high school with insatiable angst and needed to vent through my LiveJournal. Entries were mostly about AP Calculus tests and my impending graduation. I made friends and joined groups. I even sold a few art pieces. But between the college transition, my relationship with the blog ended with her desperate longing.

It wasn't until 2007 that blogging became the next new thing. Curious Tribe was born, and I fell in love. Always a fan of the written word, I was head over feet in creative expression. Updating infrequently, I posted about dope songs and videos I liked on YouTube. And with new writers and a growing following, I became more infatuated.

More posts. More writers. More content. And we got it. More readers. More responsibility. More hours recycling posts from other sites.

Our passionate love had turned out to be nothing more than cold and lonely monotony. I was going through the motions of being creative, without actually writing new content. And that was the entire reason why I started the site: to fulfill this innate desire

IF YOU LOVE HER, LET HER GO. AND IF SHE COMES BACK TO YOU, SHE PROBABLY JUST WANTS YOUR BRAINS.

to change the world with words and pictures.

Blogging died. And I killed her by wanting all the wrong things. I killed her by wanting to grow more than I wanted to create.

And now she's stalking me, back from the dead. Clawing at every new endeavor. Begging me to update her daily with articles I've read on other sites. And when I deny her, she runs to other blogs. Regurgitating the same content stolen from some unknown, unnamed source (probably the dying print industry).

So now I'm back to the basics. Learning to create again. One project a time. Setting clear goals, making real timelines, but primarily focusing on the process and not just the end result.

If you love her, let her go. And if she comes back to you, she probably just wants your brains.

It's okay to tell people what made you smile while you were surfing from work. But it's better to take the time and create something that can inspire someone else. 💣

LAST CALL

ASHLEY CHAPMAN

You've lost the cork to the California sparkling wine you received from the alcoholic uncle as a gift. This means you must finish it tonight. It will lose all its bubbly in a few.

Contemplating the repercussions of drinking the whole bottle alone, you are reminded that you are once again alone. With your scarf-covered head against the eggshell wall in disinterested melancholy, you stare at the muted television.

A white chubby girl from London sings jazz. Her songs remind you of all the problems that keep your champagne flute at hand.

Your sleek black cell phone alerts you to a text message from an old friend. "Que pasa" the text reads. You don't reply, knowing the text conversation will bring you no closer to your goal of conquering his full attention. You want more than passing inquiries.

Feeling tension in your lower back from your depressed posture, you decide to lie down in hopes that sleep will come quickly. You down another glass quickly, look around for pills to speed up the goal. No more Vicodin, codeine, nor a measly Tylenol.

Turning off the television and the exhausting jazz vocalist, you remove all your clothing except your panties and sit at the edge of the bed with your head on your knees. You whisper a prayer for love and hope that God hears it. Sure to cover your breasts and feet, you close your eyes and wait for the colored circles to stop and the dreams to begin. 💣

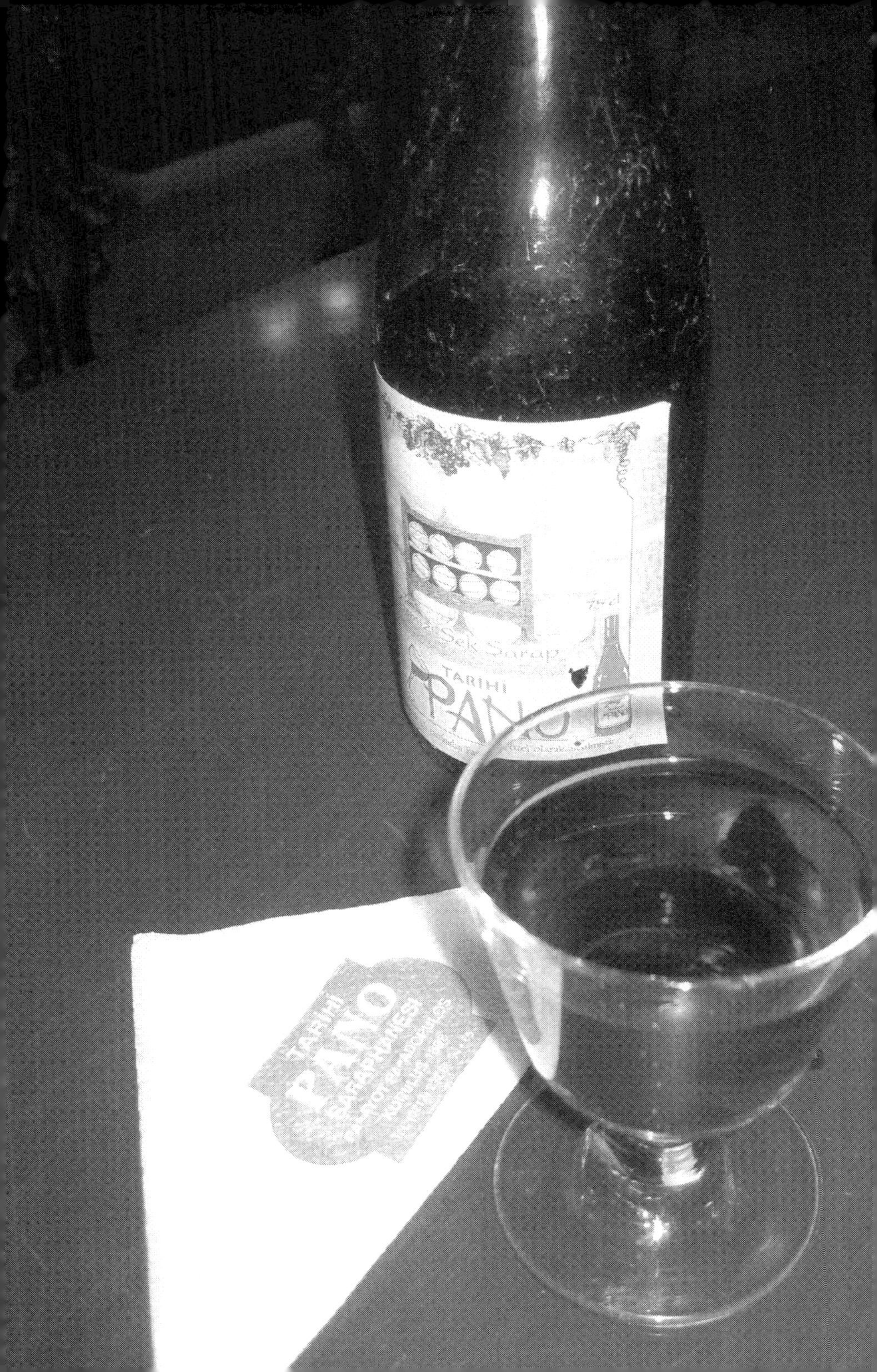
Sek Şarap
TARIHI
PANO
TARIHI
PANO
ŞARAPHANESİ

Image via: Lizzie Ford-Madrid
http://lizziefordmadrid.com

DOMESTIC

ANNA FARINAS

Marriage? Pfff...please. I'm too independent, too picky, and too selfish to be tied down to one man for "as long as we both shall live." Don't get me wrong; I believe in commitment, a bond that isn't easily broken.

I believe in the investment that the heart makes in another person, a kindred spirit whose investment is just as big as yours. But marriage is just a piece of paper. Who would give a piece of paper such authority over their lives? I would never. That was me, through high school, through undergrad. Until I met him.

Now, before your eyes roll right out of their sockets, I want to say that this is not a love story. I'm not going to tell you how we met, or about our first kiss, or how he proposed. No, this is different.

When we were "dating," (we mostly skipped this phase, as we're both relationship people. I use "dating" to refer to the time after we met and before we moved in together: about a year and a half) I insisted on everything being split 50/50. If it was my turn to take us out and my funds were low, I'd cook the burgers and bring the movie to the house. I didn't want him to have anything to hold over me if we split up. When we got engaged, we were living together, so I loosened up a bit on the half-and-half business. Honestly, it felt good to be pampered, and I could tell that it made him proud to treat me. To keep a balance, there was no shortage of pampering from my end. It felt good for me, too. Now that we're married, and our finances are combined, I hold the reins; he was happy to relinquish them. "Just give me an allowance," he said. "Twenty bucks a week's all I need," he said.

I've become a better cook, too. In the dating phase, we sought out every new and exciting restaurant in Dallas, and if the food was good, it was a bonus. It was more about being out and about. Since we've started living together, I've become a much better cook, and meals at home are treasured. Meatloaf, pies, casseroles, cobblers, the elusive homemade shrimp n' grits, cornbread, beef stew, adobo, pansit, and many more things came out of my subconscious. My culinary horizons didn't expand out of boredom. Hell, I could have fish and rice every night and would probably never tire of it. No, I wanted to cook new things for my husband. I love it when he comes home, gets a whiff of what's on the stove, and can't help but get handsy at the stove. (Too much, I know.) There's something about cooking something hot for someone you love that can swell up your own heart.

Well, I said this wasn't a love story. And yet, it is. It's about how love is transformative. It is an entity that can change everyone it touches. The hardest of hearts, the most cynical, the loneliest. Here's the interesting part: once it comes into your life and rearranges it, there are no more excuses you can make for not doing what it wants you to. Things don't make sense, and they just don't have to. 💣

Image via: Lizzie Ford-Madrid
http://lizziefordmadrid.com

LOOKING FOR LOVE IN ALL THE WRONG PLACES

CATE ROOT

Living in New Orleans is like sleeping with someone that you're pretty sure is trying to poison you. There are the clues: the barely veiled threats, the cleaning chemicals left on the countertop, the mysteriously missing neighborhood pets.

You spend the day debating what your lover could unleash on you, but night turns over and the sex haze makes you forget that you might not wake up tomorrow. You share a bed with someone you can't trust because, at some point, you forgot that there was another way to live.

It feels childish, but I've kept a running list of everything this city has ever taken away from me. It goes like this: a car, an iPod, Chanel and Betsey Johnson sunglasses, my favorite purse, a Parisian cigarette case, a computer, my lovingly archived music collection, more cell phones than I can count, and

SOMETIMES YOU FALL IN LOVE BEFORE YOU KNOW FOR SURE WHETHER OR NOT IT'S A GOOD IDEA.

I wrote some version of that paragraph over two years ago. I'd been in New Orleans for eight months, and I still just didn't get it. I felt like the awkward girl at the club, smiling at the music but unable to catch the beat. The only things I knew about this city was that I loved it, but it scared me sometimes.

Experts say that relationships usually hit a rocky period after about three years. Couples have a make-it-or-break-it crisis. And I have to tell you, NOLA and I aren't doing so well right now.

three digital cameras. Some days I add "faith" and "innocence" to that list.

I've started making noise about leaving, but I can feel NOLA's advances just around the corner. Soon, it will cool. We'll have the sweet woos of Halloween, and her parade of madness like an amuse-bouche before the celebratory feast of the holidays. I'll stop in to snowy Kansas City for Christmas and marvel at how frost hangs in the air. And then before I know it, like every damn year, Mardi Gras' beads and congas will sweep me off my feet.

What can I say? We've had a rough year. Sometimes you fall in love before you know for sure whether or not it's a good idea. You find yourself under a canopy of banana trees, the night sweetened by jasmine, and the air kissing you just enough to cool your glistening forehead.

It isn't until the morning heat latches on that you feel anxiety pitch in your belly. The flat waxy leaves of the banana tree bring no relief from humidity's vacuum. The leftover jasmine sours your stomach, and wild plans of escape dance on your tongue.

I can't tell you how many times I've decided to leave New Orleans. I feel like I'm always watching what I say about her. If I tell people about the gunshots, the blood stains, the debt, the despair, the vacancy in her eyes sometimes... what would they think? They would want me to leave her. It's the only sensible thing; it's for the best.

And yet, after a couple of weeks... something changes. There's something different about the air. NOLA and I can make a fresh start. We're following our dreams. We'll move to a new house and hope our old problems don't follow us there. We can make it, I promise. We can't just give up on love. 💣

NOBODY GIVES A SHIT ABOUT YOU BEING TIRED.

DO IT ANYWAY.

MORAL OF THE DAY

Made in the USA
Charleston, SC
14 March 2011